The Sides of Heaven
A Memoir

The fish dwell in the depths of the waters, and the eagles in the sides of heaven. One, though high, may be reached with the arrow; the other, though deep, with the hook. However the heart of man, no matter how close, cannot be known.

Burmese Proverb

The Sides of Heaven

© Hazel Barker 2018

Published by Armour Books
P. O. Box 492, Corinda QLD 4075

Cover Photos: © kasto - Can Stock Photo Inc; © Anke - Can Stock Photo Inc
Typeset by Book Whispers

ISBN: 978-1-925380-10-1

 A catalogue record for this book is available from the National Library of Australia

All rights reserved. No part of this publication may be reproduced, stored in, or introduced into a retrieval system, or transmitted, in any form, or by any means (electronic, mechanical, photocopying, recording or otherwise) without the written permission of the publisher.

The Sides of Heaven
A Memoir

Hazel Barker

Contents

Acknowledgments		1
Chapter 1	Post-war Rangoon	3
Chapter 2	Civil War	16
Chapter 3	Fear	22
Chapter 4	The Long Wait	29
Chapter 5	The Escape	36
Chapter 6	Freedom	43
Chapter 7	The Call	48
Chapter 8	Another death	56
Chapter 9	The Columban Nuns	61
Chapter 10	In Transition	64
Chapter 11	The Novitiate	67
Chapter 12	Rules and Regulations	73
Chapter 13	A Novice at last	80
Chapter 14	Lashio	87
Chapter 15	Farewell to Bertie	94
Chapter 16	Back in the Novitiate	99
Chapter 17	Home	109
Chapter 18	Taunggyi	114
Chapter 19	Disillusioned	121
Chapter 20	The Storm	130
Chapter 21	Partings	139
Chapter 22	All Alone	145
Chapter 23	Perth	151
Chapter 24	The Family	161
Chapter 25	Love	164
Chapter 26	Canberra, 1971	174
Epilogue		178

This book is dedicated

*In loving memory
Of my brother,
Peter Clive White,
Who peacefully passed away at Perth
On the nineteenth July, two thousand and eight*

Acknowledgments

The Sides of Heaven is based on my own experience, intensive research and wide-ranging interviews. However, the names of characters, other than well-known personalities have been changed.

I am deeply indebted to my husband, Colin, who patiently and painstakingly read through my drafts and was my severest critic. Without his patience and loving support, this book would have been an impossible task.

My heartfelt thanks to my brothers, Clive and Robin, and my sister, Maxine, for reminding me of incidents we experienced in our childhood and our youth, which had lain hidden in the recesses of my memory, and for important dates I had forgotten.

Finally, I wish to thank my writing groups for their helpful critiques and suggestions as I ploughed my way through the second part of my memoirs.

Chapter 1

Post-war Rangoon

Dad lied to us.

The Second World War was over, the long wait for freedom at an end. Government employees were summoned to Rangoon, and my father appointed Assistant Registrar and Personal Secretary to the Chief Justice of the Supreme Court. No accommodation was available as many homes had been bombed during the war, so he was ordered to leave us behind at Mandalay.

After suffering the lash of his tongue and feeling his blows, we regarded the separation from him as a glimpse of heaven. Our relief was to be short-lived. In late 1946 Dad wrote to Mum telling her to join him in Rangoon as a home now awaited us. All our happiness vanished.

Reluctantly, we took the train to Rangoon, only to find there *was* no house. Seven of us had to live in a single-roomed warehouse within the grounds of the High Court.

He deliberately lied so that we would have to leave Mandalay and be reunited with him.

***

During the Japanese invasion of Burma in 1941, we had evacuated up-country to Katha, in North Burma. Japanese troops pushed the British army from Burma into India, and it seemed we had been deserted.

Nourished on books during those terrible years of the war, and having three siblings older than me, I acquired a mind mature for my age.

A devout Catholic, Mum had been attracted by my father's captivating ways and fallen for him—even though he was a Muslim. All his charm disappeared once she signed the marriage certificate. What could she do? If she ran away, society would shun her. So, with the birth of each child, the chains on her tightened until they completely weighed her down.

Now she found herself with a broken heart.

Soon after our arrival in Rangoon, my brothers Rupert and Bertie commenced university studies. Rupert enrolled for his BSc. Bertie loved mathematics and had always dreamed of being an engineer. Obtaining a high score in the entrance exam, he was offered a chance to study medicine. So, to please his father, who hoped for one of his sons to qualify as a doctor, Bertie enrolled in the course.

For months, I remained at this warehouse with Mum, my brother Herman, who had infantile paralysis from birth, and Rose my young sister. Schools hadn't yet re-opened in Rangoon.

One cold December morning when Bertie had already left for the university, Rupert said, 'My neck hurts. My head is being pulled backwards.'

An Anglo-Indian caretaker lived nearby in the flat above the storeroom with his wife and two daughters so I teased him. 'Is it pulling you in the direction of the girls?'

Rupert half-smiled and shook his head, then went to bed. My brother was a keen student and never missed classes.

Remorse at teasing him tore at my heart. I knelt beside him. 'Would you like me to massage your neck?'

Rupert placed my hand on his neck, indicating where the pain lay. I rubbed it with Tiger Balm.

That tragic day unrolls before my eyes even now. Powerless to do anything, as Bertie had already left for the university and Dad was at the law court and couldn't be disturbed, Mum prayed and wrung her hands.

By the time Dad returned, Rupert grimaced in pain, unable to speak. His eyes betrayed his agony.

Dad rushed him to hospital by gharry—a horse-drawn carriage on four wheels—but when they arrived, no doctors or medical specialists were available. They were working in military hospitals, where they cared for wounded and broken prisoners-of-war flown out from Japanese concentration camps.

My brother had to make do with the understaffed hospital facilities. The nurse on duty informed my father that Rupert may not last the night. Despite the dreadful news, he did not send for Mum, but remained in hospital with Rupert. While we spent an anxious, sleepless night at home, Rupert passed away in the wee hours of the morning.

Dad returned home, his features set and the lines on his forehead more pronounced. 'Rupert died.'

Mum gasped and turned pale. 'Is he at the hospital?'

'He's in the hospital mortuary. Get dressed and come quickly.'

I glanced at Bertie. He stood transfixed, his normally cheerful smile erased. Dad beckoned a gharry.

Once we'd all squeezed into the vehicle, Mum asked, 'What did Rupert die of? He was in such pain and couldn't unclench his jaw.'

My father gazed out of the window. 'Hospitals are over-crowded in post-war Burma, so no tests were taken. Staff suspected tetanus because of his locked mandible.'

When we arrived at the hospital, we followed him in a daze as he entered the building. The smell of disinfectant hung in the rooms like a curtain. Nurses in neat white uniforms and caps flitted past noiselessly in rubber-soled shoes. The hushed silence overwhelmed me.

We passed along an endless corridor that led to the mortuary. Finally, we came to a large room with a plain concrete floor and walls. The air chilled as we entered. Corpses lay covered in white sheets with only their feet visible. Each one had a tag attached on the big toe.

I drew my coat closer to my body and shivered.

Dad jerked his chin in the direction where Rupert lay covered with a white sheet. We hurried over to him. He appeared to be sleeping peacefully with a smile on his lips. No tell-tale signs betrayed his recent agony.

Mum kissed Rupert on his forehead. 'He's pain-free and at peace now.'

'Yes,' Dad replied. 'As soon as his breathing stopped, he relaxed. I had his head cradled in my arms.'

Mum shuddered. I knew she wanted to have been beside him at his death. Yet she dared not rebuke my father.

'I'll just make a phone call to let the relatives know.' Dad moved off, leaving us standing in the cold, damp morgue. His footsteps echoed on the concrete floor.

No sooner had he disappeared down the corridor than Mum peeled back the blanket covering Rupert's torso. A brown mark a little above his waist stood out distinctly. 'Rupert still has the scar from the belting your father gave him,' she sobbed.

I placed my hand upon it, feeling the slightly raised welt. My thoughts flew back to the day my brother had received the thrashing that had scarred him for life. We'd fled for refuge during the Japanese advance to Kyauktongyi, a village in northern Burma. Darkness fell and Rupert still hadn't come home from a walk in the jungle. Frightened, we wondered whether a Japanese patrol had captured him, or a tiger devoured him.

On Rupert's return, Dad took out his anger in a ferocious attack that remained etched in our memories and on Rupert's body until this terrible day.

Mum kissed Rupert, and turned to Bertie, who nodded at me. We imitated her, each giving Rupert a kiss on his forehead. I shuddered. His forehead was icy cold; even colder than my sister June's when she'd died in Mandalay during the war.

Numbed with disbelief, none of us shed a tear. It was all so sudden, so unexpected.

My father returned in a couple of hours, smelling of alcohol. He spoke through gritted teeth. 'The undertaker will be coming to prepare him for the burial. I'll take you home now.' He turned to Bertie. 'You may remain here with the body.'

Is he referring to Rupert as 'the body'? How can he speak of his son in such a callous manner? Devastated by yet another death in the family, I wondered why Rupert had survived the threat of a Japanese sword, the attacks of malaria, and explosions from bombs and land mines, only to die now.

My brother had just entered university and been studying with zealous fervour, but his young life had been extinguished. Snuffed out like the light from a candle. All was darkness.

I consoled myself that I still had Bertie—my brother a year younger than Rupert and four years older than me.

'God has punished me for not marrying in church,' Mum moaned.

Then she showed a sudden surge of hope. 'Perhaps Rupert's death will bring about a change of heart in your father and he'll give up his drinking habits. He may even allow me to practise my religion and go to church.'

Mum prayed and fasted. She stopped using make-up, hoping God would hear her prayers. Over the ensuing years, her health gradually diminished like a tree with its bark destroyed.

***

Mum knew the importance of education. Despite her ongoing grief, when St Philomena's Girls' High School reopened, she asked Bertie to take me on his bicycle and get me enrolled. Dad grumbled at the cost of the fees, but allowed Bertie to drop me off each morning on his way to the university. Gaunt and stunted from the sickness and starvation I'd suffered during the war, I was not too heavy to take pillion riding, even for such a long distance.

The girls at school were much older than I was. They spoke about their boyfriends and the fun they had at cinemas and parties. If only I were allowed to enjoy life as they did!

Jeanette took a liking to me, and at lunchtime, we walked in the school grounds. 'Hazel…' She tossed her long chestnut hair. 'I'm in love with a soldier who wants to marry me.'

My eyes opened wide in amazement. She was only 13!

Her hazel eyes danced. 'I like speaking to you. You're a good listener and don't gossip.' After a pause, she went on, 'Who's that good-looking guy who brings you to school on his bicycle?'

I smiled. 'That's my brother.'

'Everyone thinks he's your boyfriend.'

'I don't have one.' Too ashamed to admit my father made sure I never met anyone from the opposite sex, my face burned. 'He coaches me in mathematics and teaches me how to draw contour maps for my geography homework.'

'You're lucky to have such a good brother,' Jeanette said. 'I'm always quarrelling with mine.'

The freedom and friends at school gave me a glimpse of joy. I loved school, but was unable to compensate for the years of interrupted education, even though I had attended school for eighteen months at Mandalay soon after the war.

Months passed. Eventually, Rose joined me at St Philomena's. We had no idea when the Branch Convent would re-open for primary school students. We went by bus.

Towards the end of term, our teacher selected me for the school concert. I was to pose in a pair of shorts, holding a tennis racquet while the chorus sang, 'If ever I marry again.' *Will my father buy the costume and prop for me? He always complained about the lack of money.*

In the end, I was spared the pain of asking him to get them.

The school principal watched us rehearse and cancelled the performance. 'It's sentimental slush!'

We all grumbled and called her narrow-minded behind her back. I was disappointed—but also relieved.

In April 1947, we moved to government quarters similar to the ones we had at the outbreak of war. However, instead of having the house to ourselves, we shared it with another family. We had a common stairway, bathroom and toilet, with only two bedrooms upstairs and a lounge and dining room downstairs. Bertie shared a bedroom with Herman, who had been born with infantile paralysis. The rest of us slept on the floor in one room; my parents under one mosquito net. Rose and I shared another.

At nights, after drinking his bottle of grog downstairs in the lounge,

Dad staggered up the stairs and placed a sheet over the mosquito net dividing our beds. Still awake when he climbed into bed, I heard heavy breathing and suppressed moans. *What torture is he inflicting on Mum to make her moan in that manner?* I lay, biting my lip and praying for her.

I said nothing about it, knowing she never liked us to witness her suffering.

Within a few months, Mum fell ill in the mornings. She couldn't have breakfast, and, at times, I heard her retching in the bathroom. She put on weight and her waist line grew bigger.

On my birthday, in April, Mum gave me a copy of *Martin Chuzzlewit*. 'Happy Birthday, Hazel. I have something to tell you.'

I straightaway thought of what she'd told me on my last birthday at Mandalay: that my father had tried to arrange a marriage for me with my cousin Henry. 'Not another proposal?'

Mum smiled. 'Not this time... You'll be having a new brother or sister.'

'Oh Mum!' Although she'd been putting on weight, my mother looked worn out, and hadn't yet recovered from our famine days. *Is Mum strong enough to bear a child?*

She took my hand and placed my ear close to her stomach. 'Listen to the baby's heartbeat.'

Mum continued to remain at home with Herman, while Rose went to school with me by public transport. In early January, by the time Mum was ready to give birth, the midwife arrived.

'Take Rose and Hazel for a walk on the Strand,' my father said to Bertie.

Apart from school, he never allowed me to go out without him, so what was happening? Mum's groans reached me as I left, in an agony of suspense, with Bertie and Rose. *Was she going to die?*

Bertie's brow puckered in a frown. We were both silent. Mum had grown weak since the war. I knew that she was in great danger but I didn't know anything about childbirth, except that it caused a lot of pain. Bertie said nothing, because in those days no one spoke about such matters.

After wandering around the docks for hours, we returned home. I rushed to Mum, who lay in bed, pale and weak, with a baby beside her. Beads of perspiration stood on her brow. Mum had told me the doctor would have to cut her stomach to get the baby. *Surely it left her with a wound?* I searched for bloodstained linen, but saw none. 'Show me your stitches, Mum.'

'There's no wound.' She moved her blanket and exposed her abdomen.

Mum's stomach was flabby like a deflated balloon. 'Did the baby come out of your navel?'

'Who told you that babies were born from navels?'

'Nobody. I figured it out by myself.'

Mum smiled, but remained quiet.

Named Winston after the much-loved war hero, Winston Churchill, Baby became the darling of the family—so beautiful and healthy, without having been through the trauma of hostilities to tarnish his happiness.

Soon primary schools re-opened in Rangoon, and Mum took Rose to the Branch Convent. It was only a few blocks away from home. I stayed back from school that day to take care of Winston.

On her return, Mum was flushed with excitement. 'I met the principal and, after enrolling Rose in the primary school, I told her that I used to teach in St Paul's down the road. She asked whether I was qualified, crossed herself and said, *Deo gratias*. Then she said the nuns had been praying for staff. They were so short of them as Mrs Miller, the head kindergarten teacher, died during the war. She asked me whether I could teach at their branch convent. I told her I had a baby at home. Maybe we could hire a nanny but I'd have to get my husband's permission. The nun clasped her hands together and praised the Lord. I hurried home to give you the news. I hope your father will let me work. It would be lovely to be with the nuns and teach the little ones, like old times.'

I was so glad to see Mum happy. She rarely smiled ever since we came back to join my father in Rangoon. With her salary coming in, I hoped we could hire a servant and live as we did in pre-war days—buy a car, go to cinemas and have picnics on Sundays.

Mum waited to break the news to my father, but told me she held very little hope of his consent. Hearing him unlock the front door on his return from work, she hastened towards him. I hurried after her.

'How was your day?' he asked.

'I've enrolled Rose at the primary school. They're short of staff and have begged me to work for them.'

'We could do with the extra money, but who will look after the baby?' My father looked around at our makeshift furniture of empty wooden crates.

'Couldn't we get a nanny like we did in pre-war days?' Mum asked.

'Definitely not,' he snapped. 'Their wages are too high, and our house is far too small. We don't have enough room. Besides, we'd have to feed her as well. Don't be ridiculous!'

He swung away, treating the matter as closed.

Mum's shoulders drooped. While he went for a shower and shave, she turned to me. 'He kept me locked in the house during the early days of our marriage because of his fierce jealousy. I'd love to have *some* freedom but should have known he'd never give his consent.'

That evening after dinner, while my father remained downstairs drinking and we were alone upstairs, Mum placed her hand upon my shoulder. 'Your father says I may teach.'

'So glad for you,' I exclaimed, delighted she wouldn't be locked in the house when everyone was out. 'We're getting a nanny after all?'

Mum shook her head. 'He says that *you* must look after the baby.'

'But I'm going to school. And just made a few friends. I'm too young to stop studying.'

'You could study at home and sit for your matriculation exam as a private candidate later on. Bertie will help you in geometry and arithmetic. I'll teach you algebra, and get you the text books and study guides.'

'Am I to be stuck here all day? School is my only chance of going out and socialising.'

'Then I can't teach,' Mum said. 'Your father is adamant about it. He stopped me just now and said that we need to buy some material to make new frocks for myself. Then he said, "You may accept the job on one condition." When I asked him what that was, he said, "Hazel must leave school and look after the baby. She can do something for the family until I marry her off." When I pleaded that you're so young and haven't yet completed your schooling, he said, "She may study at home. The high school is too far off. Besides, we can't afford to pay the fees as well as her bus fare. It's your choice."'

Mum paused, and a look of sorrow passed over her face. 'If you *insist* in going to school, I won't take the job.'

The whole burden of making the sacrifice now lay upon me. Mum loved teaching, but I was so happy at school with my new friends and didn't want to leave.

As I struggled with my thoughts, Mum broke in. 'It won't be *forever*, Hazel. It'll give me a chance to make contacts and perhaps one day we'll be able to get away from your father and be freed from his cruelty.'

'If you don't leave him before I'm twenty-one and of age, I'll go on my own.'

'Then you'll take care of Baby?'

I nodded, although my heart rebelled at the thought. It was only Mum's promise of freedom that made me capitulate.

'I'll make it worthwhile,' Mum promised, kissing me.

My stomach clenched, imagining myself forever at home, the uneducated daughter kept as a servant in the house. *Someone has to look after the baby, but why does it have to be me? Why can't my parents get a nanny?*

I was withdrawn from school without even a chance to say goodbye to Jeanette and my other friends. I groaned inwardly, vowing to run away—to be free from this oppression someday. The idea grew in intensity with each passing day. As the rising sun diffuses light and heat on to the earth's surface, the thought of freedom strengthened until it scorched itself into my brain. I remained inconsolable, and vowed to free myself from my father's clutches.

Mum taught me how to prepare the baby's formula and give him his bottle at fixed times. 'If he cries, check his nappy and change it, if necessary.

After lunch, give Baby a bath and croon him to sleep. He won't need much attention, so you'll have plenty of time to study.'

Looking back now, I realise what a studious child I was. No one supervised my studies in English or history. I used the study guides for English, and went through all the answers for the previous matriculation questions for history, my two favourite subjects. Mum helped me with algebra, and Bertie taught me how to read and construct contour maps.

'You always get asked to draw one in geography for the matriculation exam,' he advised me. 'Master them, and you'll pass your exam, for sure.'

Whenever in difficulties in Geometry or Arithmetic, Bertie solved the problems and taught me how to deal with them. None of the sums were too difficult for him. I admired him for his patience when explaining things.

Mum used to say, 'Bertie is gifted in maths. He should be an engineer, not a doctor. As a child he'd build bridges and buildings with his meccano set.'

But it was too late. He had already enrolled in the medical course, which was three years longer than an engineering one.

Mum left for work at eight, and I took charge of Winston until she returned at three. She and Rose walked to school, only a few blocks off. Bertie fed Herman before he left for the university, and caught a bus to be in time for lectures.

I remained at home with Baby and Herman, who could neither walk nor talk. Herman was too big for me to handle, and was entirely in Bertie's care. Whenever he soiled himself during the day, he stayed dirty until Bertie returned home and cleaned up the smelly mess.

I sympathised with Bertie, and wouldn't have changed places with him for anything in the world. He was always so kind, never saying a harsh word to Herman.

A car picked my father up in the mornings, at half past nine. He would leave home, looking very elegant in his white tropical suit. He had his own *peon*, office boy, who came to the door and carried his attaché case to the waiting car.

One sweltering hot day in July, my father dashed home from work with beads of sweat sprinkled on his forehead. He tugged at his tie even before he'd entered his dressing room. I'd never seen him like that before.

Brushing past us, he walked straight to Mum. 'Aung San has been assassinated and most of his cabinet eliminated while at a meeting. Abdul Razak, a Muslim member of Parliament, and his bodyguard also died in the shooting. The Muslims will rise and avenge this. There'll be civil war.'

'What's going to happen to us now?' Mum turned pale. She followed him upstairs, and I never got to know the end of their conversation.

I was too young to understand the implications of the political situation in Burma, but at the same time, I realised that things were not looking good for us.

Bertie, as usual, briefed me on the situation. He told me of racial riots during pre-war days in Rangoon when the Burmese had attacked Indian workers. 'Once on our way to school at St Paul's, rioters stopped a rickshaw and ordered an Anglo-Indian teacher to get off. Then they hacked off the rickshaw-man's head.'

I gasped, and Bertie continued.

'Blood spurted from his body. His head rolled on the road, leaving a red trail. We didn't stop to look any further. Teachers, who were standing in the school grounds, called out to us and we dashed off to them. They locked the gates behind us. During these Muslim-Hindu riots, Muslims tortured cows and drove the half-crazed animals into Hindu temples. Hindus retaliated by driving pigs into mosques and killing Muslims.'

'What will happen if riots break out now?'

'I don't know,' Bertie said. 'But last January, after signing an agreement with Prime Minister Atlee for independence within a year, Aung San met with ethnic leaders and persuaded them to join the Union of Burma. His party won a landslide victory in April. Only God knows what's going to happen to the country now.'

I knew that Aung San had sided with the Japanese at the start of World War II. He'd joined the Allies in the final year of hostilities and, once Japan had surrendered, he'd formed the Anti-Fascist People's League.

When Burma obtained independence from Britain in 1948, the Burmese language was made compulsory for the matriculation exam. We were Eurasians and only spoke English at home, so my knowledge of the Burmese language was very limited. Mum persuaded my father to engage a tutor for me in that subject. He grudgingly consented and, with the help of the school, Mum found one.

Acne scars pitted the tutor's face. He had a squint, making it difficult to know whether he was directing a question at me or exclaiming to himself, but he was a good teacher. My knowledge steadily improved.

I fed Winston and washed his nappies. When he demanded attention, I carried him and sat on the rocker with a book in my hand.

I wanted to be free of my father, and longed for independence—to be like my peers—to go to parties, dress in lovely clothes, wear make-up and meet boys. Mum had taught me sewing and I made my own dresses but, unlike the ones my friends wore, they weren't fashionable. My whole existence consisted of studying and baby-sitting. I looked after baby Winston and studied day and night. I loved my little brother, but I needed to meet other girls and boys.

How much longer could I endure this?

Chapter 2

Civil War

Nine months after attaining independence, civil war erupted in Burma. That year on Christmas day, local Burmese militia attacked a Karen congregation during a Church service, killing eighty people. At the same time, they marched into Christian villages and killed hundreds of Karens.

Years later, I read *Life's Journey in Faith* by Saw Spencer Zan. In it the author mentions a secret government directive to eliminate Karen army and civil officers that some high-ranking Karen officials had inadvertently discovered.

In retaliation, Karens formed the Karen National Defence Organization to protect their villages. They also sent a contingent of KNDOs to Insein, where many Karens lived. This town was just thirty kilometres away from downtown Rangoon. The rebellion surged only a short distance from our home. Life in Rangoon was unstable—half the surrounding area was in the hands of either the Karens or the Communists. Shells thundered in the distance. The capital was on the brink of falling. Top government officials fled to safety in an area surrounded by a five-metre barbed wire fence patrolled by armed guards.

My fear of war and its subsequent suffering rose once more, bringing a sour taste to my mouth. I flinched at the least noise, thinking it was a burst of shell fire.

About the same time, fighting broke out in Mandalay. The KNDOs occupied the city and demanded a separate Karen state stretching to the border of Thailand.

The Red Flag Trotskyites, the White Flag Communists, Burmese Army deserters, and the Kachin Independence Army (the KIA) also revolted against the government. In 1949, Chinese Nationalists—remnants of Chiang Kai-shek's forces who had been driven into Burma from Red China—joined in the fighting as well.

The Rangoon/Mandalay train was frequently attacked and derailed. Travel within the country was disrupted. We feared for our future. To be more secure in his job, my father took out Burmese citizenship as he now worked for the Burmese government.

Despite the civil war, I continued studying. My life went on in relentless monotony. Only the seasons changed. By May, low, black clouds drifted across the heavens, blocking out the sun. The sky pressed down upon us until the monsoons arrived and the rain beat in torrents against the windows. Time dragged its heavy chains. The clock on the wall ticked off each succeeding second.

The days were long and tedious. On and on went the drudgery. My father left for work later than Mum, and returned at five. When Mum came home in the afternoon, after refreshing herself with a cup of tea and a biscuit, she gave private tuition to backward students, while I cared for my little brother.

At nights, fear replaced boredom when my father took to the bottle, the fiery liquid adding fuel to his already overheated brain. A few drinks seemed to steal every trace of reason from him. A raised eyebrow or a timorous glance, or even silence, sent him into a bellowing rage. We trembled, afraid to speak or to move.

I vividly recall the evening Bertie crept upstairs, knocked before entering the bedroom and whispered to Mum. I don't know what he said, but I'd never seen her so angry.

Mum's face reddened. Her lips flattened as she slipped into her dressing gown. 'I'll go down and catch him in the act.'

'Then he'll know I told you.'

'Never mind.'

I followed them to the bannisters, but she turned to us. 'Remain here.' We watched Mum tiptoe down the stairs and throw open the little door under the staircase where we stored our brooms. Her voice rose in anger.

How did she dare speak to her husband like that? Will he bash her up? I never knew what happened afterwards, but I lay awake biting my lips for what seemed like hours.

The next day, Mum said, 'Your father was in the broom cupboard with the neighbour's servant girl. She's only twelve. It's a criminal offence. If he's ever found out, he'll lose his job.'

Too dumbfounded to say anything, I wondered what he was doing to the girl in that dusty broom cupboard. *Why couldn't he have taken her to the sitting room?*

Things became even worse from then on. My father left the girl alone but turned his attentions towards me. One morning after Mum and Rose had left for school, and Bertie was at the university, he said, 'Ta Ta, Hazel.' Then he reached out and drew me towards himself. His lips sought mine. I turned my head away and his wet, slimy mouth landed on my cheek.

As soon as the door closed upon him, I raced to the bathroom and scrubbed my face. I washed his spittle, lathering layers of soap on my skin and trying to scrape off his kiss, realising it was not a paternal one.

He had never displayed any affection for me as a child. I remembered the time during the war when sirens had wailed and he'd said, 'Go into the trench first, and drive away the snakes.'

If he loved me, he'd have protected me and not sent me ahead to get bitten instead.

As I was washing the dishes after dinner, my father gave me a box of chocolates. I took it reluctantly, feeling that nothing could wipe away his obnoxious kiss.

That night he reeled with alcohol. 'You've been rude to me.' His words came with a slap.

My face burned.

Circumstances were conspiring to entrap me. Bertie and I studied downstairs in the dining room while my father sat drinking in the lounge. Bertie often retired upstairs before me, while I remained to complete the work I'd set myself.

When I'd finished my studies one evening and was about to ascend the stairs, my father staggered up the hallway and kissed me. His alcoholic breath and wet, slimy kisses were revolting. Too afraid to push him away, I turned my face from him. His mouth landed on my cheek.

This occurred each night after that. I was in a dilemma. If I stopped my studies at night, I'd be unable to pass my exams and would be incapable of earning a living.

I complained to Mum.

She called Bertie aside. 'Never leave your sister alone with her father. Please remain downstairs with her when she studies at night.'

Bertie looked at me searchingly, but said nothing. After that, he stayed downstairs until I'd finished studying and retired for the night. From then on, I was able to study without further molestation.

Winter brought cooler weather and a relief from the humid monsoons. When Bertie's Christmas holidays began, we put up the Christmas tree and hung streamers from the ceiling. A week before Christmas, my father returned from work with a storm-clouded face. He banged the door shut, flung the newspapers on the table, and knocked a vase of flowers over. He had obviously been brooding the whole day. We sensed the oppression—the stifled air of a thunderstorm about to unleash its fury. Mum prayed for the threatening storm to dissipate, hoping he'd grab a bottle and drink himself into oblivion.

When I finished my studies for the night and went upstairs, he exploded and vented his spleen upon Bertie. My father's raised voice rose up to us from downstairs. Sensing danger, Mum and I strained to hear what was going on. A bitter taste rose to my mouth.

He stumbled upstairs, clutching a *dah* in his right hand, dragging it along behind him. We cowered, in a vain attempt to dissolve into the shadows. He stormed into the room and gazed at the Christmas tree. Gaily wrapped gifts lay beneath it. Red and green streamers festooned the walls and ceiling. Lifting the weapon above his head, he started a rampage of slashing, cutting and tearing the decorations until the place resembled a bloodstained battlefield.

He held the *dah* aloft and bellowed, 'There'll be no more Christmas in this house.'

We crept into bed, not knowing whether we'd live to see another day.

The next morning at breakfast, Bertie was nowhere to be seen.

My father banged his fist upon the table. 'He's not to come here again. If I catch any of you speaking to him…' He glared at each of us in turn. His unspoken threat was worse than words.

When he left for work, I rushed into Bertie's room. His bed had not been slept in.

Bertie came in to collect his things a few days later. He described what had happened that night. 'Dad seized the *dah* and attempted to run it through me.'

I gasped, and glanced up at the wall where it hung. Displayed on the dining room wall was the *dah*, a long and lethal ceremonial sword.

'I picked up a chair to defend myself, and moved around like a lion tamer warding off a beast. Dad's face was dark and threatening. The veins on his forehead stood out. His eyes shot out flames of hate. Showering curses on me he said, "Get out and never dare return or even contact your mother or sister again." I left with only the clothes I wore and walked up and down the street. If either Mum or you screamed, I meant to return and defend you. I stayed there until the house lights went off. Then I knocked at the door of a family friend, and asked for a night's shelter.'

'Where are you staying now?'

His face twisted in grief. 'With the Samuels.'

I flung my arms around Bertie and wept as he left, perhaps forever.

The memory of that night remained a recurring nightmare for a long time. Terrified, I brooded on the fate awaiting me. *Now that Bertie has gone, who'll protect me from my father's rages? His sexual harassment?* Mum would be unable to help me. I slumped into a backwash of despair. I'd sunk to the depths of hopelessness when June and Rupert had died, but my mother's faith had lifted my spirits to a level from where I could crawl back and hope for better times. Bertie's unlimited cheerfulness too had been an anchor to me over the years. Now he was no longer with us! The only peace I had was when my father was at work. I saw no future for myself until I was twenty-one and legally free to leave home. *That appeared a lifetime away! Could I last that long?*

Chapter 3

Fear

I feared my father's attention and could only move away each time he pinched my bottom or brushed his body against mine whenever he passed. Feeling naked beneath his gaze and desecrated by his touch, I avoided him and only spoke when absolutely necessary. My behaviour seemed to arouse his passions even more. I expected Mum to protect me and was aggrieved over her silence, not realising she was afraid of a bashing.

The war years in Burma had been a nightmare of hide-and-seek from the fighting and the bombing. In those days I had dared anticipate a better life, but now no hope remained. I decided to put an end to my existence. My misery had accumulated over what seemed a long life—I'd just entered my teens—and I talked myself into taking this desperate remedy to stop my endless agony.

We had a large water tank within the house, just below the high ceiling. Scrambling up, I swayed like a drunkard teetering on his toes. On reaching the tank, I sat poised on the water's edge, brushed away the cobwebs from my face and took a deep breath. I shut my eyes, contemplating my end before slipping into the water. *Is there a life after death or will I face total oblivion?*

A sudden cry broke the silence. Winston had awakened from his afternoon nap. My love for my little brother overcame my longing to escape. I snapped to attention, climbed down from the water tank and hurried to him.

After soothing him, I pondered on what would have occurred if I *did* drown myself. I imagined it all and pictured Mum returning from work hours later. *She hears Baby crying for his feed. She panics, searching every room for me. Helpless, with no one to turn to and no telephone in the house, she walks up and down carrying him in her arms until my father comes home.*

He roars with anger, accusing her of hiding me. Denial is useless. He raises his fist and strikes her. She whimpers in pain and fear.

Days pass. At the first sign of a foul odour from the water, my father climbs up to check whether a dead rat had fallen into it, and discovers my body. I'd cheated him of his incestuous desires, but is it fair to impose this added agony on my mother? She has no happiness in life except us. All her joy had been strangled since her marriage.

I finally decided to join the Rebel Army. *The Karen National Defence Organisation is fighting for their freedom. I'll enlist with them and become a heroine like Joan of Arc. If I leave a letter telling Mum of my plan, she'll be spared any reprisals.* Little did I realise that my escape would entail trekking across mountains and navigating winding rivers.

I didn't reveal to anyone what I'd contemplated doing that day and simply brooded in silence. Anger and despair seethed in my heart.

During weekends, my father took long walks, visiting friends or going by bus to the university to visit his sister Jhan and her children. Those days were a bit more tolerable. Rose always accompanied him. Now that both Rupert and June had died, he poured all his love upon her; the only child left who'd inherited his looks.

On her return from a walk one day, my sister said, 'Dad asked me, *Whom do you love? Your mother or me?*'

'What did you say?'

'I said, *I love both.*' In her childish ignorance of his true character, Rose returned his affection fully but, as each month crept by, she came to witness more and more of his cruelty.

I was pleased to have time alone with Mum when my father went out. Those hours with my mother and little brother were serene and a close bond held us together in our sorrow. On Sundays, I'd watch our neighbours walk past on their way to the Cathedral for Mass. My father never allowed us to attend Church, but I yearned for social contact and longed to do as other girls did.

Mum taught me dancing. She waltzed around the room with me, reliving the good old days, but I remained unhappy, considering it a farce. *Why learn dancing when I never have the opportunity to go to a dance or attend a party?*

My mind was peopled with stirring and gallant figures belonging to the world of romance. Like Cinderella, I wanted to dance my way to freedom. Where was my prince?

While washing the dishes and dreaming of *Romeo and Juliet*, which I was studying for my exams, I was jolted from my dreams on hearing my father's voice.

'Hazel is looking rather pale these days. She needs fresh air and exercise. I'll take her for a walk before breakfast.'

'Good idea.' Mum always tried every opportunity to send me outdoors.

I froze. My eyes dropped to the patterned linoleum flooring, wondering whether Rose would accompany me.

Later that evening, she said, 'Your father will be taking you out in the mornings. The exercise will be good for you.'

'Are you coming?' I asked, glad of the chance of being in the fresh air.

'No. I have to get ready for work.'

'But I don't want to go out alone with him.'

'You have no choice,' Mum said, 'You'll just have to make the best of it.'

My blood boiled. *My own mother was throwing me into my father's arms.* I hated those mornings and walked along in silence, kicking the occasional stone on the road, venting my frustration upon it.

My father would stop at a local teashop. 'Like some *nan roti* and cream?' He knew I had a sweet tooth.

I nodded, then stared at the waitress wiping a table with a dirty dishcloth. I listened to the customers giving orders. When the waiter brought breakfast, I broke the hot Indian bread with my fingers and scooped up a dollop of cream with it, wiping the residue off my lips.

I took care not to look at my father. I didn't want him to see the pleasure in my eyes. I shuddered, regarding the food as a bribe and thinking of the times he had kissed me with drooling lips. Mum had taught me that only my husband should ever kiss me on my mouth. It reinforced my opinion he was doing an evil thing.

Having made no progress, my father stopped taking me out in the mornings. However, during weekends, he took me boating in the Kokine lakes.

Filled with apprehension for my safety, I prayed for God's protection. *I'd have felt safer if Rose was with me. Why didn't he bring her along? What ulterior purpose did he have in mind?* The breezes stirring the grass only accentuated my helplessness in a world deaf and blind to my fear.

Couples sailed their boats, skimming like swallows over the lake. The waves lapped the sides of our boat as their laughter reached me. I longed to be out sailing with a handsome boy, enjoying a sweet romance. But here I was, swamped by fear of my father. *Why had he ignored me before? Now that I am no longer a child, he is taking a sudden interest in me like the villains in books!*

I had no respite and dreaded, not only the nights and mornings alone with him, but weekends too. For safety, I slept with a large hammer beneath my pillow. Had the slightest opportunity of taking my father's life arisen, I'd have done so without hesitation, knowing God would forgive me because *He who understands, forgives.*

I went about my chores, fantasising ways to kill my father. I considered poison and played with the thought of stabbing him with a kitchen knife. *What if I failed? He would bash me within an inch of my life. If I did succeed, how could I hide the deed?*

My mind turned to our dog, Rover. During the war, we had adopted the chocolate-coloured pup, and he'd brought us bones the butcher had flung to him. We were starving. Bertie would open the long bones and share the marrow with us, then give the bone back to our pet.

Immediately after hostilities between Japanese troops and allied forces, Rover had brought the bones of dead soldiers, hoping we would partake in his spoils just as we used to. *But Rover had gorged himself to death on the corpses, and couldn't help me dispose of the body. If he were still here, he would solve one of my problems.*

Perhaps I'd cut the corpse into little pieces. In my desperation, the sin of patricide did not deter me, but fear of discovery held me back.

One night I dreamed I was on a bridge, carrying a sack dripping with blood from my father's remains. I walked to the middle, gazed into the depths of the angry waters and looked around. *No one in sight.* I drew out one piece of the body at a time, and threw them into the river, each in a different direction and as far as possible. I bent to wash my hands, now reddened with congealed blood. Then I picked up the sack and checked the riverbanks. A figure scurried away. *There had been a witness!*

The dream ended. I awoke in a cold sweat. *Perhaps it was a warning from God.*

I resorted to praying that my father would die and release us from our bondage. Desperate, I said to Mum, 'I'm praying for his death. That's the only way we'll get rid of him.'

Mum shook her head. 'Vengeance is the Lord's.'

Looking back now, I thank the Lord for restraining me. But how desperate I must have been if murder seemed the sole solution at the time!

Mum became pregnant again, so my father requested a larger living space from the government. We were allocated a flat in Sparks Street and moved into our new home. I wondered how Bertie would get to know our current address. Ever since he had been sent away, I'd only seen him once—when he came to collect his clothes and blankets. Even then, he hardly stayed for fear his father would return from work and kill me for having let him in.

I spent the next few months in abject misery.

One evening, we had a visit from one of my father's old school mates, Mr Kirkham. We seldom had any visitors, so I tried to listen to their conversation, but only overheard a few snippets.

'Your son wants to return home, but he'd like to be baptised.' Mr Kirkham was my father's senior at work.

I couldn't hear the reply, but the next day Bertie returned. My father had never allowed us to be baptised or attend Church Services, and knew he'd be able to prevent Bertie's baptism if he accepted him back. *Perhaps that is what turned the tide in Bertie's favour.*

I shook with excitement when Bertie entered the house, glad to have my beloved brother back. But now he could *not* get baptised.

Bertie borrowed books for me from two libraries. From the British Information Service library, he brought me all the old classics by Charles Dickens and Walter Scott. From the United States Information Service, he took books like *Uncle Tom's Cabin* and *Huckleberry Finn*. I particularly loved to read James Fennimore Cooper's Leather-stocking series such as *The Deerslayer*, *The Last of the Mohicans*, *Hawk Eye* and *The Pathfinder*. When reading, I escaped into another world and lived life to the full. Books carried me away to far-off lands, and gave me the adventure, love and romance I craved.

My days continued as if nothing had happened. My father now rarely spoke to either of us. Due to Mum's advancing years and starvation during the war, she had problems from the very start of her pregnancy. Yet she walked to school every day, and continued working until the baby was nearly due.

It was a difficult labour. Mum gave birth to her youngest child, Trevor, in November 1949 at the age of forty-eight.

Trevor had big, brown eyes like Mum. Winston, now a toddler, loved his little brother. I adored the two of them. My father bought a cane cradle for Trevor. After lunch, I would sit on the rocking chair with Winston in my arms and rock Trevor's cradle with my foot. I'd softly sing the lullabies Mum used to sing to me. I'd grown attractive and did not want to waste my youth locked away, unable to taste the sweet nectar of life. I imagined myself on the bridge of life with an unhappy childhood on one side and spinsterhood on the other. *Will my days pass without tasting freedom, travel and romance?*

Mum stayed home for a few weeks after the birth. Due to the scarcity of teachers, the nuns permitted me to take over Mum's class while she was on maternity leave. She had an infant class of thirty-five students. Before Rose and I left for school, Mum prepared the day's lessons for the children and explained in detail what to do.

On my first day, a senior teacher introduced me to the children, who rose in one body and sang out, 'Good Morning, Miss.'

The double desks were arranged in neat rows with two children at each desk. They were dressed in their school uniforms; the girls in navy blue gym slips and the boys in the same coloured shorts with white shirts. A blackboard faced the class. I wrote a few words on the board as Mum had told me, revised the alphabet and taught simple words like *cat* and *bat*. Then we sang nursery rhymes.

The senior teacher sometimes came in to check on me. Embarrassed by her presence, I became self-conscious and resented her intrusion, though I now realise she was only doing her job by keeping me under supervision.

After the lunch-hour break, the children placed their heads upon their desks and had a nap. Mum said it would give help them relax and settle down before they commenced their afternoon session.

I rang a little brass bell when it was time to commence lessons. They awoke in fine spirits. At times snot dribbled down their noses. If I wasn't quick enough to wipe it off with my handkerchief, they'd smear it on their faces with the back of their hands. I hated holding their snotty hands and guiding them when they had difficulty writing. It left my palms sticky. At the same time, I was delighted to have a brief respite from domestic duties for a few weeks.

All too soon, Mum resumed teaching. I had hoped to return to school when Winston grew older, but now my hopes were crushed.

I had yet another baby brother to care for.

Chapter 4

The Long Wait

In 1942, when my family had evacuated up north to escape the advancing Japanese, we had stayed in a concentration camp in the midst of the jungle. Mum had prayed for our safety and trusted in God's providence. Now, while the terrors of war had gone, the traumas at home continued. I'll never forget the time my father picked up a piece of timber and struck Mum across her back. The loud thud mingled with her cry of pain. I closed my eyes and gritted my teeth as anguish ripped through me.

'You stood near the window and spoke loudly to attract the neighbours,' he told her.

In those days, men ruled and women wept. Mum couldn't avoid his brutality or run away and hide. She put her faith solely in God, waiting for deliverance. Over the years she became more dominated. Finally, a look of resigned sorrow banished the smile from her face.

'We will not be abandoned by God,' Mum said, through gritted teeth. 'Better to put up with misery in this world than be condemned to eternal damnation in the next.'

In her sorrow and loneliness, Mum told me of the early days of her marriage before we'd been born. Dad had made her life unbearable, casting so many false accusations at her that, in desperation, she'd swallowed a whole bottle of iodine. 'Afraid to lose my life as well as my soul,' she said, 'I raced along the streets to the nearest physician with your father in hot pursuit.'

I shuddered. 'What happened then?'

'The doctor gave me an emetic and I vomited into the wash stand.'
'Was Dad any kinder to you afterwards?'
'No. He was the same as before. But thank God, I hadn't died then. I'd have gone straight to hell, you know.'

***

My father directed our destiny with a relentless eye, destroying all chances of happiness. I had always feared him, but now I hated him. Ever since June's death, in 1944, I became withdrawn and taciturn. Now that my father kept me from attending school, I retired even further into my shell. I couldn't drag myself away from memories of life with my sister, June. Glimpses of far-off moments of bliss as a child tantalised me with their faint glimmers of past happiness.

Interspersed with these thoughts, my mind lingered on events that still fill me with dread. Even now, my mind replays one particular incident like an old film.

I sit naked in the bathroom beside an earthenware jar filled with water and pour the cool, clear liquid over me. My nipples stand out like little buttons. I soap myself, using a cake of Sunlight soap. Not the local made gritty ones we had used during the war. The lather is soft on my skin. I don't stint. The creamy substance turns to froth, releasing a faint fragrance.

I hear the patter of Rosie's feet. She's nearly four now. 'Mummy, Mummy, Daddy's peeping at Hazel.'

My father is peering in through a hole made by shrapnel in the bathroom wall!

I grab what's left of our old towel and wrap myself, not even waiting to wash off the soap suds, and open the bathroom door.

How many other times had he been peering at me having a shower?

Rose is sobbing in Mum's arms. I raise my eyebrows, mouthing the words, 'What happened?'

Mum's lips form the words: 'Tell you later.'

When my father goes out, Mum says, 'He slapped Rose for telling on him.'

My mouth flies open in surprise. He had never hit her before.

That evening, he threw all his loose change to Rose as compensation for slapping her. She picked them up in a daze and forgave him instantly.

Rose told me about it later. His actions must have taught her that you could do or say anything to a person, provided you compensated them for it later. It was this example she followed when she grew up.

***

Mum drew on her deep wells of fortitude. She wrote to the nuns where she had attended boarding school as a young girl at Mandalay, asking if they would give her refuge if things at home became intolerable.

When the Sisters replied, Mum said, 'The nuns will spare a couple of rooms for us to live at their Old Folks' Home but say that Herman is too old for their orphanage.'

Herman was the only obstacle to our freedom now.

Mum bided her time. She had to hand all her salary to her husband. He did the shopping, making sure she depended on him for everything. It was hard to put money aside with my father constantly preying on her. Nothing escaped his eye.

After a long day's work, Mum gave private tuition to some of her students, hiding the money away before he returned home. Little by little, her resources started to build up. Still, she couldn't pluck up enough courage to leave.

The days grew warmer. Just before the monsoons broke, on 24 May 1950, newspaper headlines reported: *Insein retaken by government forces.*

Another blow to freedom! We did not know then, but during the night, KNDO forces had left their stronghold in Insein, knowing they couldn't hold the town any longer.

Government forces recaptured Mandalay sometime later. They also cleared the Karens out of Syriam, a town on the opposite bank of the Rangoon River, just two kilometres from Rangoon itself.

***

My friend Colleen Soord made plans to leave for England in 1950, two years after Burma attained independence from British rule. Like us, her family had survived World War II but they had been in Mandalay during the fighting between Government and KNDO forces. The Civil War was more than they could take.

My sister and I visited Colleen at the Strand Hotel, just before her family left for London. This momentous occasion was one of the few times I was allowed out of the house. The hotel was one of the most luxurious in the British Empire. I paused before the massive marble pillars and recalled the times when, as a child, we had walked past and I'd peered in, marvelling at its magnificent marble floors.

English voices drifted towards us. Haughty doormen stood at the entrance.

We stepped in and passed an army of butlers as we made our way to Colleen's room. My heart was wrenched at her impending departure and I feared I'd never see her again.

Our visit was not long enough. Colleen and her family left on the *SS Salween*, sailing via the Suez Canal. In the ensuing years, we corresponded frequently with each other, and she sent me souvenirs from England, keeping alive my longing for liberty.

***

My eyes often strayed to Mum, who held the keys for our freedom. She found joy in teaching. She also secretly paid for Rose's ballet lessons, knowing Dad would never consent to a daughter learning dancing. Rose enjoyed herself with friends at school, but I passed my teenage years frustrated and unhappy. Life only seemed to get worse with the beatings and the debauchery. Confined to the house, the minutes dragged.

Only a few milestones marked times of joy. I passed the matriculation examination in the Second Division and was carried away on a white water-raft of excitement.

Apart from that, life continued with endless upbraidings and beatings. The locked door constrained me and terror paralysed my limbs. The scars of the body can be forgotten once the pain ceases, but a mental scar remains forever. Never to be erased. Mental torment has the power to break even the most defiant soldier. It can lead a teenager to despair and self-destruction—complete obliteration. Home was a prison.

Every night my father sat drinking a bottle of spirits, offering sips to Winston and Trevor. At times he shouted, 'Come, drink.'

I can still picture the two infants toddling over to take a sip. When the alcohol burned their tender throats, they pulled faces. My father laughed. Anger burned within me. I balled my fists and choked back my tears. *Perhaps he wants to make them alcoholics.*

It must have broken Bertie's heart to see all this. I'm sure my father's actions aroused my brother's protective instincts, but he hid his feelings beneath a carefree exterior. Years later, we were to witness Bertie's unswerving sense of duty and loyalty to the family.

Brilliant at university, he passed his exams without any great effort, but finding no heart for his studies, he sometimes failed to attend lectures. Good-looking and well-built, everyone called him *Za Lai* or 'the film star'. He often stood with his head thrown back, one hand on his hip, the conscious pride of possessing good looks imparting confidence to his tone, demeanour and deportment. Success did not inflate Bertie, nor did misfortunes deflate him. Neither arrogant nor aggressive, he loved life.

On completion of his fourth year at university, life became intolerable. My father constantly picked fault with him, threatening to throw him out of the house. One night, when in a dark mood—only two years after he'd first sent Bertie away from home—my father again threw him out. This time my brother took all his clothes with him before leaving.

When the echoes of the door closing on Bertie died, they continued to resound in my ears like an ominous prediction. I was left in total ignorance of his whereabouts. His departure cut a deep ravine in my mind and, like a raging torrent, fear rushed through me. I imagined Mum beaten into a pulp and myself as the victim of incest.

When Bertie left home, I was bereft of books and once more plunged into despair. I fretted and fumed so much Mum allowed me to go to the library after she returned from school, while my father was still at work. She always insisted I take Trevor in his pram, while Winston toddled along beside me. Sometimes Rose accompanied us.

Mum risked getting beaten up for allowing me out of the house. However, she knew my father wouldn't be too hard on her if I had my two little brothers with me, as men would think *I* was the mother, and leave me alone.

The British Council Library was a ten-minute walk. I only had to cross Merchant Street with its wide avenue of trees and continue walking for a block on Sparks Street, then turn right into Strand Road across from the Rangoon River. The library stood a few metres further on.

After Bertie's departure, my father fed and cleaned Herman, but he hired a charwoman to wash the soiled linen. I gnawed at my nails, fearing to be given charge of taking care of my crippled brother. However, Mum said he was too old for a young girl to manage.

Herman missed Bertie and shrieked for him in the stillness of the night. He constantly broke the silence with his moans. They grew fainter each night and dwindled to a mere whimper. Our hearts ached to hear the poor boy's cries.

My father dosed Herman on Aspro to keep him quiet.

Mum feared to protest openly, but whispered, 'He's going to kill the child.'

Within a few weeks, on 27 August 1951, Herman died. No one mourned him. He had suffered long enough. He lay peacefully in death, his twisted limbs now straight and relaxed—so tall and thin. I'd always thought of him as a child, but, lying stretched out on the bed, he appeared even taller than me.

Mum said, 'He probably died from an overdose of Aspro, but there is nothing we can do about it.'

No obstacle now stood in the way of our freedom. Still, afraid of being caught and dragged back, Mum hesitated. I resented her procrastination.

Alone at home, babysitting my two little brothers, reading was my only solace. The famous words of Patrick Henry, '*Give me liberty or give me death*' became my goal.

Besides the longing to escape, two emotions filled my breast—fear and hate. My father controlled the whole family with the barbed hand of a tyrant. To have whispered that word would have been to invite disaster. His anger would have been unleashed like an avalanche, burying me beneath a mountainside of falling debris.

What could I do? Hope eluded me. Why are we staying behind with my father when so many others had left the country and escaped to freedom? Why can't we run away and flee to England or Australia? The unanswered question threw me into despair.

***

By 1951, the Burmese government regained the Irrawaddy Plain from the KNDO. U Nu appeased the Karens by appointing their leaders to his cabinet and promising them an autonomous state within the Union of Burma. A semblance of peace returned to the country.

My life continued in turmoil. As the eldest child, I considered it my duty to shield the family from my father. I *had* to protect the younger children and take some of the burden off Mum.

Something eventually happened to stir the sleeping lioness within my mother, but by then it was almost too late.

Chapter 5

The Escape

The war had left me with great holes in my teeth. Dad was happy to let our teeth decay and took us to a dentist to have them extracted when the pain became unbearable. However, Mum believed in getting cavities filled. When a dental surgeon from Edinburgh opened a practice in Rangoon, Mum sent me to see him. She paid for the dental bills with money from her tuition fees.

Bertie had taken me to the dentist until banished from home. When he was no longer with us, Mum accompanied me to the clinic and made sure my appointments were during my father's work hours.

I soon had a crush on the good-looking young dentist. The thrill of his arm encircling my head compensated for the pain of the drill as he bored into my molars. My heart beat loud and fast whenever his eyes met mine. I dreamed of him, wondering whether he'd turn out to be my Prince Charming and save me from my prison.

One day at the surgery, Mum burst out, 'She's crazy over you.'

She couldn't have realised how embarrassed she had made me, but every time after that, the dentist gazed at me with a quizzical look in his blue eyes. Needless to say, nothing further developed.

Apart from these romantic encounters, life was a tedious grind. When I passed my matriculation exam, I begged my father to enroll me at the Teachers' Training College, for the next semester. However I knew my chances of getting his permission were slim.

As expected, he refused. 'I'll coach you in shorthand and typing and get you a job at my office. We can go to work together.'

I knew he'd never let me out of his sight to attend a college, so there was no alternative but to study shorthand. I disliked sitting in close proximity to my father while he instructed me. He leant forward, his eyes stabbing me like a rattlesnake about to strike its prey. I dreaded being alone with him. The room shrank.

Fortunately, knowing my need for protection, Mum constantly moved around on the pretext of tidying the room.

My father drank more heavily as the days passed. He developed a chronic cough and, at nights, he spat thick phlegm upon the floor. His manners grew worse, his habits disgusting. He seemed to persist in his dirty ways just to assert his power.

Mum laid a newspaper beside his bed to collect the stinking, sticky stuff. In the mornings, she said, 'Please put the paper in the bin, Hazel. I can't bear the vile thing. It would make me vomit.'

'This is disgusting,' I said, the first time Mum asked me to get rid of the filth. 'Why should *I* have to do this?'

'There's no one else, Hazel. Just can't do it myself.'

I resented this loathsome task. Fortunately, Mum had placed several layers of paper on the floor, and they had soaked up most of the phlegm.

Later on, my father broke out with a skin rash. Each morning his bed was covered by white flakes of dry skin and stank horribly. I wondered how Mum could lie in the same bed.

Whether his conscience plagued him or Satan had come to claim his own no one ever knew, but frightful dreams began to haunt my father. Late one night, I was awakened by fearful yells. Wet with perspiration as if the fires of hell raged within, he stumbled out of bed. 'The devils are here.' He stared ahead, his face stricken with fear as he stretched out a trembling finger. 'There's the sign of the devil.'

My heart knocked against my ribs as my eyes probed the darkness, searching for a horned creature.

'What sign?' Mum's gentle, soothing voice was like a healing balm to me and must have calmed my father too. He ceased shouting.

His chest heaved. 'A lighted cross.'

Once again, my eyes probed the night. *Nothing.*

The following morning, Mum said, 'Our day of deliverance is at hand.'

My heart leapt. *Was he going to die?* 'Why do you think so?'

'Emperor Constantine saw the sign of the cross in the sky during a battle, and knew he would conquer his enemy. I'm convinced that the cross your father saw is a sign from God.'

She was not wrong, but first we had to be tempered by the fires of more tribulation.

My apprehension turned to reality in mid-August, during a lull in the rains when the blades of grass trembled in the gentle breeze. One morning, just before he left for work, my father flung his arms around my shoulders and grabbed me. His whole body pressed against mine. My mouth became dry. Struggling to extricate myself, I burst into tears.

At that moment, God sent his angel to protect me. The peon knocked at our door. To my mind he was an angel in the guise of the office boy.

My father relaxed his hold and, releasing me, he hurried off to work.

God had saved me from further harassment.

Humiliated and helpless, I went about my chores, shaken by sobs. Like a robot, I fed and bathed Winston and Trevor, and rocked them to sleep. *It was impossible to live at home any longer. Something must be done before it is too late.*

When Mum returned from work, I told her, sobbing, what had happened.

That was the final straw. She had tolerated my father's behaviour with unresisting submission, but now she plucked up the courage to confront him.

That night, Mum must have accused him, because I saw him raise his hand and strike her mouth. I see it all—even now. *The two little ones stand in hushed silence and shrink back as he slaps her again and again across her mouth. Blood runs down her dress from a cut lip. Mum drops to her knees, begging for mercy. Her hair hangs all over her face, her arms held out, palms upward. Tears prick my eyes. Winston and Trevor cry. Rose and I watch— our common bond of pain drawing us closer.*

This picture can never be erased from my mind. Mum's feelings were somehow transferred to me. She did not suffer alone, I suffered with her and I still shudder whenever her image on that night surfaces once again.

Early next morning, when my father was having his daily walk, Mum took Rose in her arms. 'Can you leave your father and come with me? I cannot offer you much, and you will be poor.'

Breathless, I waited for her answer, knowing my freedom hinged on her reply.

Rose nodded, then blurted out, 'If I can't *buy* things, I could always make Christmas presents for everyone.'

In spite of all her father's gifts to her, he had failed to wean her off her love for Mum. Relief flooded my soul. *Now Mum was ready to leave our tormentor.*

That morning, exactly a year after Herman's death, Mum went to school and contacted Bertie. He'd found a job and been saving his earnings, knowing he may need to help us some day.

Fearing the worst, he hurried home. 'Are you all right Hazel?' He scanned my face.

'Yes. I'm okay. It's so wonderful to see you. How did you know?'

'Mum got in touch with me. How are you? Did he …?'

'No. He didn't. But I'm afraid of what he *may* do. Things get worse every day. As he was about to leave for work this morning, he put his arms around me and held me *so* close to his body. I couldn't escape. Just *couldn't*.'

Bertie put his arm around my shoulders. 'Sorry I wasn't there to protect you. Did he …tear off your clothes?'

'No. Thank God. He was dressed for work and about to leave, but I felt so powerless. What if he decides to … you know. How *horrible*! I can't stay here any longer.'

'You don't have to remain anymore. We'll be gone before he returns from work. I've made arrangements for all of you to leave. Mum says to start packing straight away. She'll be coming home early.'

A flood of joy enveloped me. *At last all those years of fear were coming to an end!* 'What a rock you are. I knew we could depend on you.'

The two little ones stood by with huge smiles on their faces. He embraced them. I started at the least noise, fearing someone had seen him and sent word to my father.

When Mum returned, her lip swollen from the previous night's beating, she moved about efficiently. Rose was busy selecting her best dresses and favourite toys. Bertie kept an eye on the time, realising we must be well clear of the house before our oppressor returned from work.

We couldn't take much—only what we could pack into a wooden box and a suitcase each for Mum, Bertie, Rose and me. Mum put Winston's and Trevor's clothing with hers.

Bertie hailed a gharry. Mum took a last look at the place where she had endured so much anguish and pain. Then we all piled into the vehicle. My heart was elated, but my legs were numb with fear. Stepping in, I thought of myself as Cinderella going to the ball in a chariot.

We boarded the train that night. I was desperate to leave, but fearful in case my father discovered our carriage and dragged us back from the station. Dressed in western clothing, we stood out among the other travellers. Conspicuous and vulnerable, I carried a portmanteau full of clothes and scanned the crowds for my father. Mum held the two boys. Rose clutched her dearest toys. Bertie had a suitcase in each hand and kept a wary lookout.

Will he find us even before we get on the train? Will he use his gun or his sword? Kill us, or worse, a thousand times worse, maim us? He'll strike our faces and scar us for life. I swallowed the lump in my throat and my hands tightened on the handle of my suitcase. *He'll discover us if the train does not arrive soon. Please God, let it be on time.*

The engine steamed into the station, breathing fire and panting like a woman in labour. Then it gave birth to hundreds of passengers from its belly and relaxed with a great hiss. We waited while the carriages were cleaned. Fear lurked in our hearts during the delay. I tapped my foot on the platform, impatient to get on the train.

Finally, it was time to board. Bertie found seats in the corner of a carriage from where no one could approach unawares, and settled down to wait. I leant out of the window to check whether my father was on the platform.

'Don't look. He'll see you if he's out there,' Bertie cautioned me.

I drew in my head, knocking it on the window-sill in my haste. I stole a glance at Mum. Her lips moved in silent prayer as she rocked Trevor in her arms. Rose stared into space. I wedged myself into a comfortable position.

The engine whistled and started to move. The train rattled on, its rhythm causing me to doze off.

Loud shouting in the corridor awakened me. The dull light showed a slight figure staggering along the aisle, hurling abuse at his fellow passengers, his voice slurred and incoherent. Mum tensed. Bertie's fists clenched. Mercifully, the three younger ones were sound asleep. The man lurched towards us, hanging onto the seats to steady himself. I tried to make myself as inconspicuous as possible and covered the lower half of my face with a handkerchief, hoping my father wouldn't notice me.

On he came, heading in our direction. Obviously searching for us, his head moved from side to side. He reached Bertie and grasped his shoulder. I held my breath. *Will he produce a knife and stab him?*

He stood rocking in time to the train's momentum. 'Don't hog the entire place. Leave room for others.' He sank into a spare seat.

My brother wrinkled his nose at the tell-tale odour of alcohol and left the intruder to sleep it off. I thanked God the man hadn't turned out to be my father.

***

A decade later, before departing for the UK, Bertie went to visit his father and learned what had occurred on the night of our escape. When his father had returned home from work that evening, no one opened the door for him or greeted his homecoming. Unlocking it with trembling hands, he had rushed into the bedroom. Finding a note pinned on his pillow, he read the message. Written in bold letters were the words:

The worm has turned.

Goaded by fury, he had fortified himself with alcohol and set out in search of us with a loaded gun. He banged on people's doors, threatening to blow out their brains if they didn't let him in, and demanding to know whether anyone had seen us.

According to Muslim law, if he discovered us on the day of our flight, he could punish us in any way he desired, even kill us. A wife was nothing but a mere chattel to be used or discarded at a man's pleasure.

Friends and neighbours feigned ignorance of our whereabouts, realising our danger if he discovered us. He left, ranting and raving.

They related the incident to Mum later on.

God had once again thrown His protective mantle over us, and my father failed to find us that night.

Chapter 6

Freedom

The monotonous chattering of wheels droned on as the train lumbered its way towards Mandalay. I slumped down in my seat, the rhythm and rocking of the carriage lulling me into a dream-like state. As the train rattled on, Mum smiled with satisfaction. I guessed she was thinking of the note she had pinned on Dad's pillow. Ever since the war, Mum had churned the phrases over in her mind and told me what she wanted to write in her farewell note.

'I'd like to be a fly on the wall when he reads my message,' she said, settling into the seat. 'The ticking of the clock will be the only sound that greets him on his return from work. My words will thunder throughout the house.'

Mum had been planning our escape, but couldn't have left him without any means of supporting her children. His cruel blows and barbed taunts had hurt her deeply, as though he had been twisting the dagger he had implanted into her heart. The Japanese occupation of Burma and the deaths of her eldest son and daughter had bruised, but not broken, her. Their deaths severed the knot binding my parents. Sickness and starvation had overtaken us in the last days of the war, but we had survived.

Mum's tight-lipped silences held the semblance of martyrdom. She had not dared to protest against her husband's illicit love affairs, his liaisons with the servant-girl or his flirtation with the secretary at work. Her passion for her husband had perished long ago, yet she had put up with his blows and his infidelity. Now, seated in the train, Mum's eyes, normally so sad, were dancing. We were about to commence a new life. Thanks to the Lord, our little ship now sailed on its solitary course to a favourable wind.

***

The train wheezed to a stop at Mandalay. We disembarked and, as we approached the Catholic sector of the town, a soft wind was blowing, bearing on its wings a sense of elation. Squirrels descended from the tamarind trees on either side of the road. They sat with their forelegs touching, as if in greeting. Church bells chimed a welcome. Mum stopped to say the Angelus while I breathed a silent prayer of thanksgiving. Bertie herded us into the convent grounds.

Mum let her gaze linger on the brick wall surrounding the Convent of St Joseph. 'That should be high enough to keep him out.'

Bertie jerked his head towards the massive wrought-iron gates. 'They're open now, but they'll be shut and securely locked at nights.'

Mum nodded. 'It should be quite safe for us.'

'Yes. He'll never be able to molest you here.' Bertie's glance took me in too.

Mum sighed. 'It nearly drove me insane when your father locked me in the house all those years.'

Bertie placed a protective arm around her. 'Never again, Mum. *Never again.*'

'Thank God for that.' Mum relapsed into silence, probably recalling the times we had lived opposite St Joseph's during the war and Rupert and June were with us.

My heart swelled with pride in Bertie, who stood ready to shield us from harm. I can still picture our entrance into the convent. A white statue of St Joseph stood in front of the building. A flood of confidence lit up Mum's face as she stopped and gazed at the sculpture. She had always taught us to have a special devotion to the saint who had watched over Jesus and Mary during their life on earth.

The nuns welcomed us warmly. Sister Martha, the Mother Superior, gave us a unit in the Old Folk's Home that stood within the convent grounds. The bishop provided Bertie with temporary lodgings in the rectory.

Within a few weeks, the bishop promised my brother a position as Headmaster at Tanghpre, forty kilometres north of Myitkyina.

'You may commence work after Christmas in the new year,' the Bishop said. 'The school is in a remote area where tigers roam on the hills and the occasional call of jackals stab the silence. Orchids bloom in the rain forest and bamboo grows profusely around there.'

The college had been opened for a year, and the Columban priests wanted a Headmaster to replace the priest who currently worked as Principal. This would give him time to carry out his missionary duties and visit his parishioners living in the foothills of the Himalayas.

Bertie accepted the position even though it parted him from us. I could sense the joy of freedom tingled through his veins like an elixir, bracing him for anything.

We made the most of the remaining four months, before Bertie's departure to Myitkyina. In the evenings leading up to Christmas, we boarded a truck and sang carols outside people's homes. I met boys and girls my own age and enjoyed a drop of wine and a slice of Christmas cake after the carols.

Freed at last from my father, I basked in my newly-found independence and was now at liberty to do all the things I'd long dreamed of!

Mum's younger brother, Pat, worked as a guard at Pyinmana, a major town on the Rangoon-Mandalay rail-line. He soon found me employment as a clerk in the Burma Railways. I bought a Raleigh bicycle with my first pay packet. Fortunately, I had learned to cycle as a child and now rode to work, grateful to God for our deliverance. My heart sang.

I met a good-looking young Anglo-Indian clerk at work. He often stood on the verandah and gazed at me as I cycled into the office forecourt. Once when giving me some papers at work, our hands touched, and brought on a tingling sensation—sweet and confusing. My heart leapt. I did not speak. Dared not look at him.

After that, I found myself glancing in his direction. *Was this love?*

Rose, a favourite with the nuns, adopted their pious ways. I remember the night she'd prayed longer than usual.

'Are you praying for something special?'

Rose smiled and shook her head. 'I pretend to be each one of us and say the prayer, *I lay me down to sleep.*'

The last lines ended:

And if I die before I wake,
I pray to God my soul to take.

My heart went out to my sister. The sight of her praying remains treasured in the storehouse of my memories. A flood of joy filled me. The joy of living. The joy of freedom.

Mum made her peace with God. She wanted a new life for us, and we were baptised. She had secretly christened us as babies, but we'd been denied the privilege of publicly professing our faith. We received a lot of gifts like rosaries and holy pictures from the nuns. One of them gave me a little book entitled *The Imitation of Christ* by Thomas à Kempis. It consisted of meditations on the life of Christ and instilled in me a love of prayer. The book was to have a profound effect on me. I learned to love God more and to accept His will in everything. I read the Bible from cover to cover and marvelled at the mystery of God.

Our rooms at the Old Home were not spacious, but they served as a home with no tyrant to torment us. We lived within the walls of the convent where peace and harmony prevailed. One section of the convent housed the nuns, and the other, an orphanage. I made friends with some of the orphans. They lived a secluded life. Educated by the nuns until they reached the age of seventeen, they were paired off with eligible Catholics. Many of them were unprepared for marriage.

One night an orphan-bride fled from her nuptial bed and, knocking at the Archbishop's door, gasped out that the groom was doing *terrible things* to her.

The old Archbishop, too embarrassed to enlighten her upon the secrets of matrimony, smiled. 'Good, my child. Now return to your husband.'

The bride returned to the astonished man.

Despite my father's molestations, I too remained naïve and was ignorant of the facts of life.

Chapter 7

The Call

Despite our cramped quarters within the convent walls, we were deliriously happy. Mum's two brothers, George and Pat, often came to visit us. Mum's marriage had deeply distressed them, but now, confronted by the children of that ill-fated union, they accepted us without reserve. They played the guitar and taught Bertie some chords. We soon grew to love our two uncles.

Uprooted from her old surroundings, Rose could not settle down and complained of a stomach ache every morning. Fearing she missed her father more than she cared to admit, and hoping she'd be happier among companions of her own age group, Bertie offered to pay for her fees at a boarding school run by the nuns. The convent was perched on a hill at Maymyo, some seventy kilometres from Mandalay.

Bertie escorted Rose to Maymyo, enrolled her at the school and took upon himself the responsibility of paying the boarding fees until she had completed her education. Mum realised it was best, but it tore her heart in two. She feared to travel too far from the safety of the convent in case her husband stalked her, so I went alone to visit Rose at Maymyo.

The drive up the pine-covered hills through the winding roads took me past well-kept lawns and masses of red, orange or purple bougainvillea, hibiscus, roses and flowering shrubs. The taxi dropped me off at the convent. Fallen leaves emitted the fresh odour of eucalyptus in the convent grounds. The mountain air suited Rose and gave her cheeks a rosy glow. We spent a few delightful hours together having afternoon tea and chatting.

I stayed for the night at a cousin's place, and left the next morning.

***

Mum applied for and was appointed as a teacher at the English Convent across the road from the unit where we lived. It was called the English Convent because the school curriculum was in English. Most of the nuns were French with some Anglo-Indian and Anglo-Burmese nuns.

The old ladies from the Home took care of Winston and Trevor in a child-minding centre while Mum taught. Little Winston missed Mum and, knowing she was just across the road, he raced off. With tears streaming down his face, he cried out for his mother.

A passing nun chased after Winston and tied him to a chair. 'I will untie you only if you promise not to run away again.'

Winston nodded and kept to his word.

My poor little brother! How lonely he must have been in the hands of total strangers the whole day. I'm sure it was agonising to Mum when she heard about the incident on her return.

The following year, Mum obtained a position at St Peter's, only ten minutes' walk from the convent. Winston was six by then, old enough to attend school. Their hearts must have overflowed with happiness as they proudly set out for St Peter's each day.

***

Bertie drew a substantial salary as the principal of the College at Tanghpre. A large timber structure served as a school and overlooked a garden where the students grew vegetables. The more academic students attended college, while the others learned farming methods. They also constructed a church, entirely of bamboo, under the supervision of their parish priest. Within a short space of time, Bertie formed a choir to sing God's praises in the bamboo church.

During the May school holidays, we boarded the train to Myitkyina and stayed at the college with Bertie. He proudly showed us around his school and the bamboo church his students had built. At morning tea, Bertie pointed out and named each of the birds.

The fresh mountain air and brisk walks in the country gave a fine colour to our cheeks and brought to mind our happy childhood days when June was alive and the whole family went for walks on the hills in Kalaw. The Irrawaddy River sparkled in the sun, and we loved to dabble in the icy waters. My heart filled with so much happiness it hurt. *If only we could always be together like this!* But jobs were scarce at Mandalay ever since the British government had left Burma.

After a pleasant two weeks, it was heart-wrenching to leave Bertie.

***

Unlike Tanghpre or Rangoon where it rained for nine months of the year, the sun showered sunbeams on Mandalay, enabling me to enjoy the outdoors. After work, I took Winston and Trevor for cycle rides around Fort Dufferin. Winston sat on the crossbar and Trevor at the back on the carrier. A profusion of pink and mauve lotus covered the moat. I enjoyed the cool air, and revelled in the sheer joy of being alive.

Uncle George was the parish priest in Meiktila, a town nestled near a lake. He invited us for a vacation, so I applied for a week's leave during Rose's school holiday. We boarded the train to Meiktila. While Uncle George toiled in his pastoral duties, we took walks near the tranquil lake, enjoying peace and solitude. The lake shimmered like glass in the sunset, the surrounding carpet of grass inviting us to linger. Not a breath stirred the air. The lake had been a grave for several hundred Japanese who, in 1945, had committed suicide by throwing themselves in, rather than surrender. We walked along, blissfully unaware of the ghosts of soldiers that haunted the place.

The sound of footsteps behind us broke the silence. We turned around. A native followed us. *What were his intentions? The sun was about to set and the shadows had grown longer.* Rose gripped my wrist. I shook it off. *I would need both my hands to defend the two of us if the man attacked!*

'Don't show any fear, but hurry,' I whispered.

We lengthened our strides and swung our arms to display confidence.

Heart beating furiously, I prayed for our safety and held my head high.

We arrived back safely. Perhaps the man had no evil intention and was only on the way home to his village.

***

A single lamp burned golden before the altar in the convent chapel. The stained glass windows shafted light onto the floor. Peace overwhelmed me and I kept hearing the words, 'Taste and see that the Lord is sweet.'

I wondered whether the Lord wished me to dedicate my life to Him as a nun. The Irish Columban nuns from Myitkyina had attracted me by their sense of humour and friendly manner, so I considered joining them.

A life of solitude and prayer appealed to me but, like Mum, the wings of romance at times bore me aloft, and I was reluctant to give up my freedom.

'God has called you,' my spiritual director, who was also my Father Confessor said. 'Do not hesitate to answer His call. Don't swerve from your calling.'

One weekend, the Anglo-Indian clerk from work came over to see us at the Old Folks' Home. He took a seat on one of the two chairs and Mum sat on the other. I sat on a bed, slightly embarrassed at our poor living conditions, but he didn't seem to notice. My friend invited me to his house to meet his mother who suffered from consumption. Mum must have sensed a budding romance because she encouraged me to accept the invitation.

His mother got out of bed to greet me and spoke in a soft and gentle manner.

A short time later, his parish priest visited us, quizzing me about my feelings for the young man. I guessed he'd asked the priest to act as his intermediary. Although thrilled to know I was attractive to men, I hesitated.

Mum had often told me that men changed after marriage. *Could I ever trust a man?* Having witnessed the wretched life she had led, I was reluctant to tie myself down. In the Catholic Church marriage was forever. If a man treated me as my father had behaved to my mother, I would walk out on him.

It was a struggle to go against my feelings for the young clerk. However, not wanting to give him hope, I dropped my eyes before the priest's inquiring look. 'I'm thinking of entering a convent.'

'Then what are you waiting for?' he asked. 'You shouldn't be wasting any time.'

Weeks passed with my soul in turmoil. Love of my family and the joy of freedom held me back. Besides that, I was reluctant to leave the world so soon, especially when just beginning to taste its delights.

***

Clerical duties kept me busy at work. The clicking of typewriter keys and the constant calls for the peons on the buzzer were the only sounds that reached my desk. Within a few weeks of my employment, my boss sent the office boy to summon me to his office.

When I entered, he said, 'Take a seat. How do you like the work? Have you settled in well?'

All heads turned in my direction when I returned to my desk and sat down. *Was it unusual for the boss to enquire about a new clerk's welfare?*

Another day, the boss again sent for me. 'Do you have any problems at work?'

He knew my uncle Pat, and I assumed he was taking an interest because of that.

Mum thought differently. 'He's fond of you.' Her eyes twinkled. 'So which of the two are you going to choose?'

Not long after this, my boss came to our unit. Surprised to see him at my humble home, I didn't know what to say. *Was Mum right after all? Was he courting me?*

'May I come in?' he asked.

'Of course, please do.' I led him into our tiny dwelling and introduced my mother, who shook hands and gracefully sank into a chair. Embarrassed at not being able to offer him a cup of tea or coffee, I perched myself on one of the beds.

'What are your plans for the future?' he asked. 'It does not look bright for us Anglo-Indians. I'll be leaving for the UK shortly.'

I gasped, sorry to lose such a kind and considerate employer. 'I'd like to enter a convent and dedicate myself to God.' *How strange that my boss should come to wish me goodbye!*

His eyes opened wide. 'Don't do that. It's a difficult life. You won't persevere.'

'I'll leave before my vows if it's unsuitable for me.'

'No. No. My sister tried to be a nun, found it too hard, and left. She was never the same again. She's nuts.' He looked upset, and it dawned on me that this was his way of sounding me out before proposing.

'If God calls me, I must go.'

He attempted to dissuade me, but I remained firm in my resolve, determined to enter a convent and be assured of peace in this world and in the next. His wealth did not matter to me. My choice would have been the clerk who was young and handsome, anyway.

Mum must have taken this incident as proof that I really meant to dedicate my life to God. Despite realising she'd have to support three children on her teacher's salary, she said, 'I'm honoured that God has chosen my daughter to serve Him.'

She was disappointed however that I'd chosen to join the Columban nuns and not the Sisters of St Joseph who'd given us shelter at our time of need. But Uncle George had told me the French nuns were rigid in their ways and he felt their lifestyle wouldn't suit me.

I struggled with my feelings and delayed in answering the call of God.

Within two years after Bertie's departure for Tanghpre, Trevor fell ill. Neither of us had worked long enough to obtain leave from work, so we reluctantly left him in the hands of one of the old ladies at the Home.

On my return from work, one of the orphans ran up to me. 'The doctor says that your brother has contracted diphtheria from another child.'

Trevor looked so weak. He burned with fever and struggled for breath.

Choking with sorrow, fear of losing Trevor took hold of me. I held him in my arms and paced up and down, powerless to help my little brother.

As soon as Mum entered the convent grounds, the orphans sprang the dreadful news upon her. 'Your baby is sick,' they shouted.

Mum hastened towards our little room. A string of questions were obviously trembling on her tongue. Her face broke and, holding Trevor to her breast, she wept. Her sobbing sounded like something was being torn from her heart. Trevor looked so tiny and helpless as she held him tightly to her heart.

Mum was just in time to clutch him to her breast and embrace him. He looked up at her as if in reproach for leaving him with strangers. Then he stretched out his arms to me. I took him from Mum and held him gently but, seeing Mum's pleading eyes, surrendered him to her.

Seconds later, Trevor let out a few gasps and stopped breathing. He was only four years' old. Death stole him away without warning. Taken swiftly, just like the other three children Mum had lost.

Trevor died on 15 March 1954, on the very same date June had died ten years earlier. His death re-opened the scar that had remained on my heart since her passing. I was inconsolable. *Winston had been playing with Trevor only that morning. What if he catches diphtheria and dies too? God, please spare my little Winston,* I prayed.

Trevor lay in a small, white coffin with a simple flower arrangement in perfect proportion for such a little one. Only Mum, Rose and Winston mourned his loss with me. We knelt in the chapel, eyes swollen with unshed tears, waiting for the service to begin. Overcome by sorrow, I thought of June and Rupert's deaths. *Why does death steal away my brothers and sister?*

My mind drifted to Bertie. We had sent him a telegram but he was unable to obtain leave for the funeral.

Within a few minutes, the whole community of nuns and orphans streamed into the convent chapel. The Mass was short but performed with all the solemnity customary for a departed soul.

After the service, the priest walked with long, slow strides in the cemetery. His eyes never left the ground. The wind blew his cassock and carried the sound of Mum's sobs. Her grief frozen, she stood stiffly as they lowered the little box into the gaping earth. Only her faith enabled her to accept this blow.

Rupert, June and Herman had been entombed solely with Mum's silent prayers. Trevor was the only child in our family to receive Christian rites.

With glazed eyes, I gazed at the grave and stood by Mum's side while the white coffin came to rest at the bottom of the hole.

Trevor was buried on a bright, sunny day.

One by one, the nuns approached, giving their condolences.

An old nun squeezed my hand and said, 'An angel gone up to heaven.'

My tears flowed.

Is God showing me that life is short but death eternal? Am I wrong to delay answering His call?

Rousseau had said, 'Freedom is the power to choose your own chains.'

I did exactly that.

Chapter 8

Another death

By the grace of God, little Winston did not get diphtheria.

April brought the mango showers and soon we were all feasting on the famous Mandalay *nette* mangoes. The rains cleared the dust, and the countryside remained cloaked in green. Monsoonal rains had filled a seasonal freshwater lake in Thagundiang on the outskirts of Mandalay, turning it into an idyllic spot.

Uncle Pat invited Rose and me to picnic there with his friends. How well I recall that momentous day. The scorching summer heat had departed, leaving the countryside renewed in a mantle of green. After a refreshing swim, we had lunch, rested and told stories. Uncle Pat, who loved music and singing, was the life of the party. He strummed on his guitar and sang with a strong baritone voice beneath the shade of the trees. The song he had composed in the last few months of Japanese occupation, broke the vast expanse of stillness:

> *Baby, your father is Japanese,*
> *May you never see him again,*
> *Very soon you will be*
> *On a new Dad's knee,*
> *'Twas the fault of my days gone by.*

The lyrics show that the native women who had co-habited with Japanese soldiers now looked to the victors—British or American fathers—

for their children. As the silver notes sobbed across the plain, I raised my heart in thanksgiving to the Lord, for giving us this marvellous life.

On that balmy day in autumn, as Pat sang, a cry of panic rose. A boy, who wasn't one of our party, had swum to a submerged tree in the distance, and called for help. Without hesitation, Pat dived into the lake and swam towards the teenager, who was hanging on to the topmost branches. With long powerful strokes, Pat headed for the boy and grabbed his shirt, but the victim struggled in panic and snatched at my uncle's hair in an attempt to save himself.

Worn out with the day's swimming, Pat floundered beneath the extra weight. Halfway across, his struggles became apparent but he kept going until another member of the party reached him.

'Take the lad,' Pat gasped. 'I can't make it back. Cramps!'

He continued to swim until crumpled up with pain. Eventually, he called out, 'Help, help.'

His voice carried over the water to us but no one else was a strong swimmer, capable of attempting a rescue. Helpless, we watched like moths drawn into the candle flame. Pat's cries grew fainter and fainter until they stopped. My heart clutched in fear. *Are we about to lose our uncle?*

Pat's friend staggered up the embankment, dragging the boy with him. *Will he swim back and help Pat?* No. Exhausted, he flung himself down on the bank, gasping for breath. We sped along the bank, scanning the lake, hoping we'd see Pat hanging onto one of the submerged trees.

Only the empty surface of the water greeted us. I remained speechless. My heart pounded and my breathing was ragged. A web of grief covered my mind.

Half an hour later a boat arrived and explored the lake for my uncle. We watched and prayed in silence until darkness drove us home.

Pat's body rose to the surface the next morning, and he was laid out for us to view. Mucus slowly trickled down each nostril, but he looked at peace with the world.

The muscles in my chest tightened and my chin quivered as I gazed down at his face. Pat had been orphaned at ten, and deprived of the love of his parents. Now, his teak coffin was silk-lined and he lay in the luxury he'd never enjoyed during his life.

Mum rarely met her brother after her marriage but they had kept in touch on birthdays and Christmas. My mother had hoped to see more of her brothers and make up for their years of separation, but it was not to be.

***

The weather was perfect on the day of the funeral, with the mere hint of a breeze ruffling the leaves. *If only Pat was alive*, I reflected, looking up at the cloudless sky. The church spire reached up, touching the sky with its stony finger. Friends gathered, talking in hushed voices with tears in their eyes.

Uncle George consoled us. 'Pat's one indiscretion had been drink; not violent bouts of intoxication, but a diligent application to the bottle. Reckless of life, he had performed the most daring feats in drunken bravado. He particularly loved jumping off trains while crossing over high bridges, as if the raging torrent below attracted him. I helped him overcome his drinking habits barely a few months before his demise. He made his peace with God before his death.'

On the way back from the funeral, Mum and Uncle George walked ahead. I fell into step beside them.

'Your grandfather died saving others too,' he said.

'What did he do?' I asked.

'Inspections. He was a Permanent Way Inspector in the Railways. He inspected the lines and checked their safety.'

'Yes,' Mum added. 'Dad had a section of the railway track and was provided with a trolley and two coolies.'

'Dad was quite a hero. He sacrificed himself to save others,' George said. 'During the monsoons, the track had been washed away by the rains, and the train was forced to stop a few hundred yards from the station. It would take some time for the repair-gang to arrive and another couple of hours to fix it.'

'So, Dad helped them,' Mum added, 'even in such bad weather. He used his umbrella and mackintosh to shelter the women and children.' Her eyes glistened with unshed tears.

'Once at the station everyone changed into dry clothing, but Dad neglected himself.' A sense of pride crept into George's voice. 'He went back again and again to assist the others. Dad got pneumonia and died soon after.' He sighed. 'Pat too, sacrificed his own life to save a stranger.'

For years I'd swum in a sea of darkness and in the last twelve months, I'd reached calm water. But now, with my uncle's demise soon after little Trevor's, I realised the pleasures of life were transient. The spectre of death was all too familiar to me. The past returned in waves of vivid recollection. Within the brief span of my life, I'd seen it steal away four of my siblings. June went first. Rupert died next, followed by Herman and Trevor. Uncle Pat was now with God.

A stab of pain shot through me, ripping open old wounds that had scarcely healed. I recalled the words from a book. 'What is life that one should cling to it? What is death that one should shrink from it?' Only those left behind suffered the pain and loss. The others went to receive their just desserts.

Pat's demise strengthened my resolve to enter a convent. *No longer can I ignore God's Finger pointing towards religious life. I have to go. I've waited so long for freedom. Now, I'll have to cut myself loose from familiar shores and launch out into uncharted seas with God at the helm.*

Having sailed long enough in the contending currents and tides of time, I understood the necessity of trimming my sails to the prevailing winds. My thirst for excitement and the pleasures so recently discovered made me reluctant to abandon the world. The compulsion to do His will now drew me to the convent.

My spiritual director knew about everything I'd been going through. 'Waste no time lest the devil sway you from your intention to dedicate yourself to God.'

In answer to my request to join their convent, the Columban nuns at Myitkyina suggested I spend a year or two teaching at their missionary school before entering their novitiate.

My lips quivered when my little brother Winston said, 'If you love me, how can you leave me, Hazel?'

His words were like a loving reproach and they plucked at my heart strings. Torn with grief, my mind turned back to our separation from Bertie. *How Winston must have suffered when his father figure left home. He lost his little companion Trevor, and now he was going to be parted from me.*

That night, my pillow was wet from tears. I did my best to sacrifice my baser feelings and turn my thoughts to serve the Lord.

Morning brought a renewal of hope. I had a hurried breakfast before leaving for the station. As the train left, my family stood, waving at the black smoke while I stared out of the window with tears streaming down my face.

***

The morning mist had settled on the surrounding jungle when I arrived in Myitkyina, two days' later. The convent, church and the priests' house were made of brick. Two smiling Irish nuns, Mother Andrew and Sister Ita, took me to the boarding school, a raised timber structure with a long verandah. My bed, curtained off from the boarders, occupied one corner of a dormitory. All buildings stood within sight of each other. Secure in my new home—safe from prowling tigers or two-legged intruders, I settled in immediately.

The year at Myitkyina was a happy one even though Bertie was only able to visit on weekends. Each Saturday, he drove down from Tanghpre on his motor bike and we took long drives, riding full-throttle on an abandoned airstrip. At times, we stopped beside the river or beneath a shady tree, soothed by the sound of rustling leaves. Bertie would speak of his work and sing for me as he used to, in our childhood days. As he sang, the joyous occasions of my life flooded back. I thought of my happy months in Mandalay with Mum, Rupert, Bertie and Rose, immediately after the war, when my father was away in Rangoon. The years rolled away and we were children once again.

Each night, a light in the church revealed my spiritual director, Father Howe, kneeling and praying late into the night. I vowed to do the same when in the convent. Finally I fell asleep, listening to the orchestra of the cicadas.

Chapter 9

The Columban Nuns

The highlight of my sojourn in Myitkyina was the National Eucharist Congress. Held at Rangoon in 1956, thousands of Catholics came from all over the world and converged on the metropolis to express their faith and celebrate this momentous event—the first ever in Burma. Bertie and I went by a special train with the Columban priests and their parishioners. When we stopped at Mandalay, Mum and Rose came to meet us. Rose joined us and, although Mum wanted to come to Rangoon with us too, she was afraid my father would stalk her.

The trip from Myitkyina to Rangoon took four days. In the mornings, the priest said Mass in the crowded carriage. I could almost reach out and touch the consecrated Host. An ecstasy of joy overcame me and increased the fire of my devotion, burning—so I felt—like gems of flame.

The year rolled by. The nuns suggested I wait for their Mother General from Ireland to visit Burma and have an interview with her. It dampened my resolution and made me impatient.

She finally arrived. At the end of the interview she said, 'We only have novitiates in Ireland or America. The cost of sending you to train overseas would be too prohibitive if you do not persevere.'

'But I'm sincere in my intentions.'

'We can't afford to take the risk. It's not feasible.'

'Aren't you taking any novices from Burma, Mother?'

'We're thinking of opening a novitiate for indigenous Kachin girls in the future. It wouldn't suit you. Life will be too difficult for you up here.'

This was a blow. I'd refrained from fun and parties. I'd joined the Legion of Mary, helping to bring lost sheep into the fold. A nun in all but in name, my plans to join a convent came to an abrupt halt. After soaring above the clouds, I drifted back to earth like a deflated balloon. *God is rejecting me. What does the Lord intend for me? Is it marriage? Have I lost the chance of love forever?*

My spiritual director, Father Howe, met me just outside the confessional soon after my interview with the Mother General. 'I'd like to speak to you, Hazel.' He motioned me to a pew. 'What do you intend doing with your life now?'

'To follow my vocation and be a nun. A good nun.'

'Ever contemplated marrying? Marriage is a vocation, as well. You can be faithful to God in wedded life too.'

Staring upwards, my mind drifted back to Mandalay, to Mum and the proposals I'd received.

Father Howe broke into my thoughts. 'A good Catholic boy in Myitkyina shows an interest in you.'

I bridled with indignation, unable to keep the pride from my voice. 'I've had other offers of marriage at Mandalay too.'

'What are you going to do?'

'Spend Christmas with Mum and the family to get over this disappointment. Perhaps in the new year I'll be able to think clearer again.'

'If you still want to enter a convent then, what will you do?'

'Finding a suitable order may be difficult.' There were various kinds of orders I could choose from—ones devoted to prayer or to social works like teaching, nursing, running orphanages or homes for the aged.

'Don't fear, my child,' Father Howe replied. 'God always has work for willing hands.'

'Mum would like me to join the St Joseph nuns at Mandalay.'

'I've met the Bishop and a few other priests from Mandalay, but know nothing much about the nuns.'

'St Joseph's was Mum's old school and she'd like her family close by. My sister is a boarder at Maymyo, where the nuns have a novitiate.'

'Well, after the festive season if you still desire to enter religious life, get in touch with me. There's a congregation at Toungoo in central Burma. They're semi-contemplative and are a teaching order. They would probably suit you, as you love prayer. I could help you with them and put you in contact with the Mother Superior.'

'That's wonderful. Thank you, Father.'

He looked grave. 'They are called the Sisters of Reparation. Their Mother House is in Milan.'

'What about the convent in Toungoo?'

'They run a novitiate there and have several convents over the north-eastern part of Burma. You could be posted to any of their convents in the hills among our converts once your training is over. But first, go home and have a happy and holy Christmas.'

'Thank you, Father.'

He made the Sign of the Cross above me. 'Write to me next year and, if you still feel the same, I'll start the ball rolling. Now go in peace.'

Chapter 10

In Transition

After my interview with the head of the Columban nuns, I bought a red floral carpet to refurbish the convent chapel to show there were no ill feelings. Then I bought my rail ticket for the first train home and went to wish Father Howe goodbye.

He shook hands. 'Don't spend all your money. You need to save your earnings for your dowry. The nuns at Toungoo told me you'll need to give them Ks 500 when you enter. This is necessary in case you decide to leave the convent one day. It will be returned to you then, so you won't be destitute if you should leave. If you do remain with them, they'll hold your money until your death.'

'I'll never leave on my own accord, Father.'

His eyes twinkled. 'God bless you, my child.'

Bertie drove down on his motor-bike to see me off at the station.

'Aren't you coming home for Christmas? I hoped we'd be travelling down together.'

'No such luck,' Bertie said. 'A headmaster has so much paper work and red-tape to go through ... But I'll be home for Christmas.'

My last goodbye was to the nuns. A priest had been teaching Irish dancing to me and some of the senior students, and we were to perform at a state function. The nuns were disappointed to see me leave so soon after school closed for Christmas.

'Can't you go a bit later?' the Mother Superior asked.

'It would be delightful to perform for dignitaries and then travel home with Bertie, but I'm anxious to spend as much time as possible with my family.'

***

Mindful of Father Howe's advice, I refrained from buying any Christmas presents, telling myself to get used to the idea. After all, I wouldn't be able to give them any gifts as a novice in the convent. I arrived empty-handed, feeling like I'd already taken the vow of poverty. It was wonderful to be back again. Mum was now living in the home she'd inherited from her parents. Little Winston was as sweet as ever. Rose was home from boarding school for the Christmas holidays.

Bertie joined us on Christmas Eve in time for Midnight Mass. He had gifts for everyone except me. He took my hands. 'I didn't get one for you as you'll have to leave it behind.'

'Yes. It would break my heart to leave something you'd just given me.' *To have him for Christmas was a sufficient reward.*

Rose pranced about; delighted with the costume jewellery he'd bought for her. The turquoise bracelet matched the blue of Mum's dress.

For church, Mum wore her white court shoes and white dress strewn with blue cornflowers. Bertie's voice resonated in the choir and his girlfriend sang a solo. How delightful to be all together once again!

On Christmas day, we visited friends and drank their health in damson wine. Little Winston was too young for wine, but he beamed with joy at the cakes and Christmas fare. I guessed he too, was delighted that once again, we were together.

Bertie remained with us until school re-opened the following year, then left for his job in the hills.

***

Uncle George was now the mentor of the family. The congregation at Toungoo was well-known to him and he approved of my second choice, the Sisters of Reparation. 'The nuns are mostly Italian, their lives steeped in faith and prayer,' he replied, when I wrote informing him of my decision to join them.

I looked upon my priest-uncle as a father-figure. Even though his mission was now based at Thazi in central Burma, some one hundred and eighty kilometres from Mandalay, I benefited from his fatherly advice. He wrote long letters with solemn words of advice. He had trained in Penang and told me of his gruelling time in preparation for the priesthood. 'The vow of chastity is never easy,' he warned.

Father George had a strong sense of humour and an immense faith that remained with him throughout his life. Tall and broad, he was the diametric opposite of my father in every way. Gifted with a strong bass voice, he would boom out, telling his congregation to love God and repent of their sins. He enjoyed a good joke and sang songs like *I dream of Jeannie with her light, brown hair* when among friends and family. He'd been a flirt before entering the seminary and it was rumoured that, as a student at St. Peter's, he had written love letters to every girl his age at St. Joseph's Girls' College.

A friend once asked him why he had entered the seminary.

'On a visit to Pyinmana, someone in white appeared to me in a dream and told me to be a priest. I had the same dream every night until I decided to do as I was bidden.'

George did so, and persevered in his vocation until death.

All too soon it was time to leave for Toungoo. Once again, I tore myself away from my family. A pang of guilt for leaving Mum to bear the burden of bringing up Rose and Winston on her own gripped me. But the Lord said to leave father and mother, as well as brother and sister, and follow Him. The pain of leaving little Winston wrenched my heart. My lip trembled as I wished my family goodbye for the second time.

Chapter 11

The Novitiate

As the train pulled into Toungoo station, I looked around in case a nun was there to meet me. People were curled up on benches, fast asleep. Others pushed past, carrying cases in one hand and dragging a child with the other. The station platform was strewn with litter and stained with betel juice. The sound of loud voices filled the air, but no one was there to greet me.

Fortunately, Mum had lived in Toungoo as a child, and she'd told me how to get from the station to the convent. I walked the short distance to St. Joseph's. The large wrought-iron gates set in a brick wall, encompassing the building, gave a fortress-like effect. The convent looked down from a hill at the town kneeling at its feet. An impassable barrier sheltered it from the rest of the world. A green lawn flowed down to a sports field. Stopping short at the gate, I turned around and gazed at the mountain ranges stretching to the east and the west. The hillsides had been thick with the large-leafed teak forests when, as a child, I'd passed them on our way to Kalaw. But they were too far off now to see clearly.

Shaking off all thoughts of the past, I turned and stepped up to the gates. After longing for freedom for so long, I was now voluntarily giving it up for God's love.

No sound broke the silence when I pressed a large button marked, 'Please ring.' Minutes passed. *Does the bell work? Should I try again? Perhaps not. I should not show impatience.* A matronly nun finally strode down the front steps of the main building, her rotund face unsmiling.

Her countenance lit up as she unlocked the gate and invited me in. 'I'm Sister Luke, the nursing sister. You must be Hazel.'

'Yes. I've just got in from Mandalay.' My bag contained a few dresses, some items for my personal toilet and a purse with the dowry of five hundred kyats.

The gates groaned as Sister Luke shut them and placed the key in her pocket. 'The community is at prayers at the moment. The train must have arrived earlier than expected. The Mother Superior usually sends someone to the station to meet a new aspirant.'

'Trains are never on time, are they? Fortunately, we had a good run and were not delayed. The walk didn't take long … Hope I'm not causing any inconvenience? I can wait in the garden, if you like.'

'Don't worry, my dear.' Her eyes twinkled. 'I'll show you around your new home.' She escorted me towards the main building.

The central door of the long, two-storied structure led to a flight of stairs. The nun pointed to a building at the back connected by a covered walkway. 'That's the refectory where we have our meals.'

'It's not under the same roof.' I wondered why it was apart from the living area.

'It's better this way. It keeps the Chapel and rest of the convent quiet, but everything is in close proximity.'

On reaching the top of the stairs, she glanced down at the gardens. 'The secondary and primary schools are next to our convent. The senior school is the large brick building alongside it. The junior school is at the base of the hill. They're separated by a sports field.'

'Are the pupils from both schools kept separate from each other?'

'Yes. The sports field acts as a barrier and helps to segregate the juniors from the seniors. It's on roster for the two on different days.'

'Aren't they ever allowed to be together?'

'Only during school Masses, or when they visit the Chapel privately.'

A heavy door stood in front of us, defying further progress. Sister Luke pushed it open. 'Come in.'

Overcome with awe and reverence as though in a church, I followed closely and stepped into the cool of the interior. The portal shut with a sigh that echoed along the corridor.

Once we crossed the threshold, the town no longer seemed to exist. A sacred silence pervaded. The solid panels absorbed all the noise and bustle of the outside world and gave a sense of stability and permanence. I foresaw some difficulties in the transition from ordinary life to a religious one, but felt ready for the challenge.

'At the far end of the building is the novitiate.' Sister Luke motioned her head in its direction. She led me up the stairs along a timber-floored corridor that resounded to the slightest footfall. The odour of polish arose as we entered the room. 'This is where you'll learn the Rules. The Mistress of Postulants will instruct and guide you. Only postulants and novices are allowed here. Professed nuns like me are not permitted to enter.'

Why is she in the forbidden precincts?

She must have read the question on my face. 'As the nursing sister, I care for all the sick within the premises and have the privilege of coming and going as I please.'

Chairs stood against the walls of the room. A desk and chair occupied the centre of the floor and a massive chest with coffin-like drawers towered at the far end.

'That's where the novices and postulants keep their sewing and knitting,' Sister Luke explained. 'It's similar to the professed nuns' lecture room, but you aren't allowed to go there until you've made your vows.'

The sparse surroundings looked like a hermitage. A refuge from the world.

On hearing the sound of footsteps approaching, I straightened up.

Sister Luke smiled. 'Prayers are over. I'll wait to introduce you to Mother Luigi, the Mistress of Postulants.'

My heart beat fiercely as I studied the novices and postulants. They entered noiselessly, took their sewing and knitting from the chest of drawers and sat down. I counted six novices and twelve postulants.

Mother Luigi came in next. Rosie Joseph, from Myitkyina, trailed behind. We had been in the Legion of Mary together; she'd been the secretary, and I, the treasurer.

Sister Luke introduced me to Mother Luigi, and left.

Mother Luigi presented me to the postulants. 'You'll get to know their names in time. Now I'll let Sister Therese, the most senior postulant, look after you.' Then walking towards her desk, she sat down.

Sister Therese handed me some sewing, beckoned me to take a chair and sat beside me. From time to time, a postulant came up to Mother Luigi, asking for help with her embroidery or knitting. I sat in silence, taking everything in.

The day was stifling hot. Seeing a jug of water on a side table, I was about to take a drink, when Sister Therese stopped me. 'Ask permission from the novice mistress first. You must ask permission for everything you do.'

Was I to ask permission before having a drink! No, I'd rather die. The thirst gave me a headache and my throat was parched. The headache wound its way around my skull and entered the sockets of my eyes. I considered taking the first train back, but it would make me a laughing stock among the folk at home.

Time passed. A spell of dizziness came over me. A novice approached the novice mistress, who sat sewing, rigid with glacial impassivity. She asked permission for a drink, and the novice mistress nodded her head. Swallowing my pride, I followed her example, and requested permission through tense and parched lips. The novice mistress looked up from her sewing, smiled and inclined her head in consent.

A flood of relief rushed through me. *It was not too difficult after all.*

The next day at morning lecture, the novice mistress explained that if we asked permission for something, God would bless our action. 'If you obey your novice mistress, and offer up your deeds to the Lord, you are obeying His will. Do everything for God. Recognise God's will in every microscopic detail of your life. From prayer to mere physical actions like eating or drinking.'

She told us to repeat the words, *Jesus, meek and humble of heart, make our hearts like unto Thine,* and impressed on us the necessity of saying aspirations during the day.

I had entered the convent to do God's will. A simple request sounded an easy way of obeying the Lord. But first I had to conquer myself, overcome the love of worldly music, my attachment to family and friends, and be humble. *Could I do all this and a thousand other things besides?*

Silence hung from the walls like a thick carpet, infusing every corner of the convent and penetrating my soul. Everyone walked soundlessly, closed doors gently; spoke rarely and never raised their voices above a hushed breath.

Struck by the stillness in the novitiate, I was soon to learn that the observance of this rule meant absolute silence in one's movements, including loud laughter or speech even at recreation. Everyone went about doing whatever they had to do in silence; broken only by short bursts of prayer from one or another of the novices. These prayers were aspirations, often used to recall one's thoughts to God.

In the evenings, we assembled in the novitiate for our daily recreation before the Grand Silence, which extended from eight pm until after Mass the next morning. At first, the utter quietness made me want to scream, 'Turn on the radio.'

At home, the wireless was always on and music filtered through the house. No chore at home was carried out without the accompaniment of some melody from the Bakelite box. I had sewed to the strains of *Don't Let the Stars Get in Your Eyes* and *Three Coins in a Fountain*. I'd washed and wiped the dishes to *Rock Around the Clock* with Bill Haley.

My thoughts drifted back to my sister Rose who used to sing *How Much is that Doggie in the Window* and *Rudolph the Red-nosed Reindeer*. They wandered on to my brother, Bertie. He'd strum his guitar and warble, *Dear Hearts and Gentle People, Music, Music, Music, Goodnight Irene, Beloved Be Faithful, The Tennessee Waltz, Mocking Bird Hill, Too Young,* and *The Loveliest Night of the Year*.

I knew all the words too, and would sing softly when at home. Mum's songs never failed to scoop up my courage from the pit of despair. Now, I had to silence my mind to all but the voice of God. There was to be no more singing, except to praise the Lord with hymns. Talking was only for necessities.

Mother Luigi ruled over us like a queen. Her duty was to train us in the way of perfection. She taught us to remain silent with head bowed in submission, and not excuse ourselves when corrected. She insisted on a remorseless separation from everything that did not draw us to God. Interaction with the outside world was to be cut off and replaced by communion with God.

'That means all visits and letters from friends and relatives. Newspapers and secular books or magazines are forbidden. Abandon yourself to God and remain totally detached from what goes on outside the convent walls.' Mother Luigi became our guide, philosopher and friend as well as our mother and confidante. She pointed out the importance of obeying the Rules of the Congregation in every minute detail. 'Keep your mind on God at all times. Empty it of everything but God. Never swing your arms or run, and above all don't let your eyes wander around. Custody of the eyes is of the utmost importance. Always keep them cast down.'

Every day she instilled into us the necessity of obedience and humility. Obedience was a total handing over of our life. It was a self-emptying, similar to what Christ did when He became a human being.

Mother Luigi related the story about a novice who had been told to plant a twig in the garden. 'The stick was dead but she'd been ordered to water it daily. The novice filled a bucket from the tap and, carrying it for a long distance, watered it every day. God rewarded her obedience by making the dry stick burst into bloom and grow into a tree. Now it is called the Tree of Obedience.'

I listened wide-eyed. My heart leapt. *I'd love to witness a miracle.* I'd been drawn to life in a convent after reading *The Imitation of Christ*. This was better than I'd anticipated. In a fever of enthusiasm, I made up my mind to obey the rules meticulously. How simple everything seemed!

Chapter 12

Rules and Regulations

The day after my arrival, Mother Luigi took me to meet Mother Ester and Mother Angela. Mother Ester was the most senior of the Sisters of Reparation in Burma and Mother Angela the Mother Superior of St Joseph's Convent. They kissed me on both cheeks and welcomed me into the convent.

Mother Angela assigned me a teaching position in the primary school, and gave me the necessary text books. On the first day of school, she conducted me to my classroom. She walked with the aid of a walking stick. The sound of it tapping on the floor announced her approach. All the students rose as she entered.

Thirty desks set up in neat rows and columns faced the teacher's desk. A blackboard was mounted on two legs in the front. A group of children aged about nine to ten years, stood behind their wooden desks and sang out, 'Good Morning, Mother,' in a sing-song voice.

She smiled. 'This is Miss White, who will be teaching you.'

'Good Morning, Miss,' they chanted, in the same musical manner.

The children were eager to learn, so my days at school passed without a hitch.

As the school day was from 8 am to 3 pm, I was absent from Prime and Vespers, but joined the rest of the community for the remainder of the day. I lived in the novitiate and followed the same rules as the others. The silence was as quiet as the passage of stars. Although quite strange at first, I grew to love it and gloried in a life dedicated to God.

The novices and postulants engaged in silent prayer, sewing, mending clothes and Altar cloths or vestments. I longed to embroider the beautiful motifs and flowers, but spent most of the day teaching. This only left me the week-ends free. Even then, my mind was subjected to the most rigorous discipline, as the novice mistress kept reminding us to keep a guard against worldly thoughts. To think of anything but spiritual thoughts was contrary to the rule.

'Remember, idleness is the devil's workshop,' Mother Luigi reminded us.

Along with rules controlling every aspect of life in a convent, there towered the hierarchy. A girl entered as an aspirant. After a period of about six months she was made a postulant, becoming a novice after a further six to twelve months. A novice took temporary vows for a year, and after that period renewed them for another three years. She would then choose to become a fully-fledged nun bound to God for the rest of her life, or leave the convent. She usually took her final pledge when her novitiate ended.

Each step up the ladder occurred at a set time every year. These were held either at the end of the annual retreat in January, or on a feast day.

Clothes ranged from dresses with a medal fastened to a blue ribbon for aspirants and black habits without bonnets for postulants. Novices dressed wholly in white until they pronounced their vows. Then they were vested in a heavy black habit with a white bonnet and black veil.

The beds in our dormitory were arranged in rows along the length of each wall, with two more rows in the centre. Mother Luigi slept in the corner, curtained off from us. As I was the most junior aspirant, my bed was closest to hers. Rosie was next to me. Twelve postulants and twenty-five novices occupied the rest of the dormitory. A solid brick wall separated our novitiate from the nuns' living area. Canon Law made it imperative for us to be separated from the rest of the community. The nuns and novices had different sleeping quarters but came together in the refectory or the Chapel. Even then, we were forbidden to converse with the professed nuns.

Each nun had her own private cell. It was small and sparse, but when a woman dedicated her life to God her needs were few. Her cell had a crucifix above the head of her bed, a table for a washbowl and toilet necessities, and a cupboard to store her clothes. Personal items were strictly forbidden. God was all she needed.

We had no possessions, as nuns are expected to emulate the poverty of Christ. We entered the novitiate as rich or poor, educated or ignorant. Now, united in our desire to be one with Jesus, we were equal in poverty.

A corridor outside the novitiate and the nuns' quarters ran all the way to the Chapel, where a nun or a novice took turns kneeling in prayer. Someone always prayed before the altar until the early hours of the morning, when the whole community gathered for Mass and meditation. The Altar was beautifully decorated with fresh flowers and their perfume wafted across the Chapel, the most peaceful place within the convent. Here the promise, *Come to Me all ye who labour and are burdened and I will refresh you*, revived the spirits of anyone seeking solace in God.

Our daily routine commenced at half past four each day. We woke before dawn with the ringing of a hand-bell. Mother Luigi dropped to her knees and cried, 'Praise be the Lord Jesus Christ.'

We sprang into action and knelt on the cold, bare timber floor, responding, 'Blessed be God.'

To rise without a moment's delay was the first act of self-denial demanded each morning. I hardly felt inclined to bounce out of bed at such an uninspiring hour, especially in winter, but sprang up, knowing it was God's call. Some of the novices slept soundly thorough the loud clanging of the bell, but the novice mistress repeated her cry louder and more high-pitched, until they grunted a reply from beneath the bedclothes.

We had to perform our morning ablutions and dress within ten minutes, so a long queue of novices and postulants strung out in front of the toilets. Rosie and I found it difficult to keep pace with the others and were late for prayers. Within a week, however, we learned to catch up with the rest.

We gathered on the verandah in pairs, followed Mother Luigi into the Chapel and knelt on the polished wooden pews. An aisle separated the two rows of pews. A few minutes after we arrived, a nun read the day's meditation. My eyes remained firmly fixed on the Altar or on the dangerously polished parquet floor. Despite this, my thoughts flitted like a butterfly from flower to flower and could not be pinned down. The silence was unbroken except for the whisper of a nun's habit as she shifted in her seat.

Each morning my mind wandered, unable to concentrate on the meditation. Stifling a yawn, I listened to the rain beating on the roof or the wind sighing amongst the trees. Being the most junior aspirant, the mistress of postulants gave me the seat next to her. She remained straight and upright, never touching the back of the bench. To make sure they didn't fall asleep, she would push the novices' backs away if they leaned against the seats.

I couldn't escape the playback of memories, and thoughts of my family kept recurring like an old gramophone record.

The meditation lasted for half an hour. To indicate the end, the nun in charge of the prayers for the week called out, 'Resolution,' in a loud voice.

With a sudden jolt, I fell to my knees, trying to think of a particular virtue to work on. Not having deliberately allowed my mind to stray, it was not a sin. All the same, my lack of concentration troubled me. Unused to rising so early in the mornings, this was the most difficult part of the day.

Mass followed meditation and prayers. By then, fully awake, I prayed with devotion. After Mass, we genuflected in pairs, and streamed back to the novitiate, in silence, leaving behind a solitary novice to spend one hour before the Altar. We made our beds and then swept the dormitory in silent prayer interspersed by short aspirations like *Sacred Heart of Jesus I place all my trust in Thee*. Faint with hunger, the smell of cooking drifted up from the refectory. A rumbling rose in my stomach, and my thoughts flew to hot buttered toast and strawberry jam. Little did I realise to begin with that our first meal would consist of a cup of coffee and a bowl of fried rice spooned from a large dish.

The bell for breakfast never seemed to ring. My stomach growled and pangs of hunger smote me, making me cast back my mind to the war days when we were starving. Mother Luigi had explained that, apart from a spirit of humility and obedience, prayer and sacrifice were the most valuable things in spiritual life. So I offered up my pangs of hunger to God in reparation for the sins of the world.

Victor Hugo had described the peal of bells as 'the opera of the steeples,' and I waited for their ringing each morning. The voice of the bell directed our lives and told us when to eat, sleep or go to the Chapel to pray. They were music to my ears. At the first tinkle, we stopped whatever we were doing, and hurried towards the refectory. Those who arrived late could either go up to the Mother Superior and apologise, or fall on both knees and kiss the floor at her feet.

I happened to be in the toilet once, when the breakfast bell rang. I heard the nuns' footsteps, but the call of nature was urgent and demanding. After relieving myself, I arrived late and flustered. Rather than face the Mother Superior, I kissed the floor. With downcast eyes, I hastened to my place and wiped my lips to remove any dust and grime. Even after bolting my food down, I failed to finish with the others and had to remain behind. That made me late for the lecture by the novice mistress.

At morning lectures, the girls sat in a semi-circle around Mother Luigi. The seat was hard. Uncomfortable in the wooden chair, I looked around for a cushion to ease the discomfort. There were none—they were regarded as a luxury.

'The Grand Silence starts after evening prayer. Use the time to commune with God. After Morning Prayer and Mass are you allowed to speak, but only when strictly necessary.' Mother Luigi's eyes scanned us. 'For friendly conversation we have one hour of recreation after dinner, and that is from seven to eight. You may also talk during meals on Sundays and feast days when Mother Superior rings a hand-bell to indicate that you may speak.' Here, she smiled as if to say that things were not that difficult after all. She paused a few moments to let her words sink in. 'Even at such times, you are never permitted to talk of your families or your past. *Worldly* topics *must* be avoided.'

The rules smothered me—how to walk and keep the eyes downcast, and how to ask for salt or butter at mealtimes. In short—to get permission for everything. The list seemed endless but I felt it was God's way of testing my love for Him and strove to obey each rule without a murmur.

As well as the daily lecture after breakfast, we had another at five. Mother Luigi stressed that we must practise penance and make reparation for our own sins as well as those of others. I loved to learn about God and sacrifice.

Months passed. One day, my ears pricked up and I sat up straight when she said, 'At our convent in Italy, police bring in young girls whom they find on the streets. We pray for them to turn away from their lives of degradation. Once, the police brought in a girl in a weak condition. The Mother Superior placed her in the care of a holy nun, who put her straight to bed, knelt at the bedside and prayed for her conversion. The girl appeared to slowly rise into the air like a helium balloon. Then the demon that possessed her, thundered out all manner of threats. A priest had to be called in to exorcise the evil spirit.'

Like an orator, Mother Luigi paused for effect. 'After the exorcism, the girl changed her ways and even asked to enter our novitiate. We found her a position as housemaid. She eventually married a good Catholic boy.' Mother Luigi's voice rose. 'God always answers prayers especially if accompanied by penance.'

I listened spell-bound, promising myself to excel in obedience and be a saint someday.

Once a month, we were bound to tell Mother Luigi if we had broken the rules in any way. I told her all my peccadilloes and lack of success during morning meditation. I recalled my priest-uncle warning me of the problems associated with the vow of chastity, and mentioned that sensuous desire sometimes stirred me.

The following day, Mother Luigi handed me a white calico bag containing a chain with spikes. 'Wear this around your thigh for an hour each day in a spirit of humility and penance, and God will help you. Make sure you use it for no longer than one hour daily and don't tie it too tight.'

The metal chain had been beaten flat with sharp points facing inwards so that they pierced my thigh, causing just enough pain to distract my mind and help subdue the stirrings of passion. It caused red dents in my skin but it helped. Whenever troubled by sensuous thoughts or feelings, I pressed my hand against the chain and let the sharp ends pierce my flesh. The pain distracted me from unwanted thoughts.

Years later, the novice mistress told me of a young nun who had requested the doctor for a hysterectomy while in hospital for minor surgery, because she was in acute agony every month during her periods. 'The Mother Superior was in a rage for not having been consulted, but it was too late to do anything at that stage.'

Perhaps the nun regretted her action when she left the convent and returned to the world a few years later.

It was not surprising that the nun chose to have such a procedure. I never suffered from premenstrual tension or pains, but my periods were a time of distress during the novitiate days. We were given similar sanitary napkins—a piece of white cloth hemmed all around with no initials on them. These, we had to soak in a bucket, and wash later, when time permitted.

In a novitiate with some forty novices, at least two of us were menstruating each day. As the buckets and napkins were identical, it was impossible to know mine, and I had to wash what could well have belonged to someone else. Even after hanging them out in the sun, there was no way of knowing which ones to collect from the clothes-line. It was humiliating and revolting, but considering this as one of the sacrifices of religious life, I remained silent.

Despite all these hardships, I surrendered myself to the joy of being enveloped in God's love. I volunteered to have an hour, praying alone in the chapel in the silence and solitude of night, savouring the sweetness of the Lord.

Chapter 13

A Novice at last

After two months as aspirants, we took the first step up the ladder of religious life, and were admitted as postulants. This allowed us a transition into religious life without too radical a change in dress. We discarded our lay clothing and wore black. It made us look like nuns without a bonnet.

Within six months, Rosie and I were admitted as novices and were told to invite our family members to celebrate our admission as novices. The novitiate is two years in length and consists of a canonical year and an apostolic year. A canonical year is a time of further separation from the world, deeper prayer and greater integration of religious identity. An apostolic year is when the novice is sent out of the novitiate to experience the life of missionary at a convent in one of the mission stations.

Bertie was still in Tanghpre at the time, but unable to get leave from his Headmaster's post. Mum, Rose and Winston boarded the train to Toungoo, and stayed at the convent for a few days. Overjoyed, I carried their meals to them on a tray and spent all day with my family, except when at prayer or lectures.

How quickly the days passed and how wonderful to spend time together again!

On August 15, on the feast of the Assumption of Our Lady, only eight months after entering the novitiate, I became a novice and received a habit. A nun cut my hair short and hid it beneath a bonnet. Eager to dedicate my entire life in God's service, my heart fluttered like a bird and my breathing was rapid. No sacrifice was too great for the Lord.

After the ceremony, Mum held me at arm's length and admired me in my spotless new outfit. A lump rose to my throat as I waved my family goodbye.

Mum wrote to me every week. I looked forward to her news. She told me that Bertie had found the Kachin hills too remote and lonely, so he'd resigned from his position as Headmaster at Tanghpre. After he quit, Uncle George found him an excellent position at Chauk on the oilfields.

Prayer before the Eucharist fuelled my efforts to grow in virtue and be like clay in the Hands of the Divine Potter. World events passed unnoticed during my canonical year. The only news we were told was that John XXIII became pontiff and brought about many changes in the church. The waves raised by the Pope caused a ripple-effect on missionaries in far-off Burma, giving members of religious orders permission to study for a university degree. Later on, this was to affect my life in the convent.

As I had a higher education than the other novices and postulants, the Mother Superior selected me to read in the refectory during the time the nuns ate in silence, while listening to readings from the lives of saints. Books had always been my passion and now I vowed to emulate the holy people and attain sainthood someday. The Mother Superior rang the bell to indicate when to stop and return to my place. When the bell rang a second time, all stood up to say Thanksgiving, but I remained seated and resumed my meal alone, while the others filed out.

On feast days, we were allowed to speak to each other during meals, though it pleased me more to read or listen to the readings rather than talk.

The twelve months of my canonical year were demanding. We were not permitted any contact with the outside world. In place of teaching at school, I taught English and Typing to the novices. Teaching the novices was a challenging task. Like marionettes, my colleagues sat quietly in class, obeying all instructions. They never smiled or laughed except at recreation, and appeared devoid of any sense of humour.

Rosie painted Christmas cards for the festive season, or embroidered

Altar cloths and vestments. She never had any difficult or challenging jobs such as teaching adults. I envied her, and longed to learn something beautiful and creative, too. My nails bit into the palms of my hands in an effort to control the rising anger. My pulse speeded up and my heart pounded. I struggled to curb the rebellious feelings that rose to strangle me. Despite confessing my sin in the confessional, the feeling persisted, gnawing my vitals and intruding into my prayers.

I'll never forget the day the Mistress of Novices handed me a statue of Our Lady. 'Sandpaper the faded paint.'

After cleaning and sandpapering the statue for hours, I looked forward to giving it a new coat of paint and went up to Mother Luigi, waiting for further instructions.

She handed it over to Rosie instead.

Had I been made to do the difficult and dirty work for Rosie? If they want her to paint the statue, why can't she do everything herself? Unkind thoughts took over my mind. To be denied the privilege of painting was bad enough, but I'd been given the groundwork so that she could put on the finishing touches! I bowed my head to hide my trembling lips. Consumed with resentment, and unable to shake off my uncharitable thoughts and feelings despite weekly visits to the confessional, I remained in torment.

Anger and jealousy are fatal to inner peace. The struggle against my natural reactions turned out an all-consuming job, robbing me of my former joy and peace of mind. Rosie and I had been in the Legion of Mary at Myitkyina and got on well, although we had totally different personalities. Now, her mere presence filled me with anger.

A nun is only permitted to find emotional satisfaction in devotion to God. Attachment to another is strictly taboo. If two sisters seemed to enjoy being together, the novice mistress separated them, as it was considered potentially destructive to community life and could arouse sensual feelings. The Church referred to the attraction of one nun to another as *a particular friendship*. Rose spoke fluent English, so we had often spoken to each other, but we had been warned not to single out each other's company. I used this rule as an excuse to avoid her.

Towards the end of 1957, the convent held a concert for the feast of Mother Ester, our Mother Regional. One of the professed nuns wrote a drama on her life and coached me for the part of Mother Ester as a young novice. When the day of the performance arrived, I was overcome by pride. The concert was a brief respite from a life of prayer and sacrifice, and the thought of proving my dramatic skills to the others was like balm to my hurt feelings.

The play was performed before the whole community of nuns in their common room and everyone gave a round of applause at the end of the play. I foolishly imagined they were applauding my acting, and failed to confess my sin of pride in the confessional.

Just before Christmas, several busloads of nuns arrived at the Mother House for the annual retreat. Three Anglo-Indian novices stood out among the Italian and Karen nuns. Our novice mistress, Mother Luigi, introduced us to the three senior novices— Sister Josephine, Sister Louise-Clare and Sister Irene. Sister Josephine had a roguish look on her face, and Sister Louise-Clare's glasses could not hide the twinkle in her eyes. Sister Irene had the appearance of a martyr. She spoke softly, sounded wheezy and had an air of suffering.

Were they formerly from Toungoo, or like me, did they come from elsewhere? I longed to know their ages, another taboo subject.

'Where are your convents stationed?' It was the only thing we were permitted to ask. I secretly hoped to be sent to a convent with one of them when it was my turn to leave the novitiate.

Sister Josephine said, 'Sister Irene and I are both stationed at Namtu and Sister Louise-Clare is at Taunggyi. We have ten days of prayer and silence here before taking our final vows. Please pray for us.'

'Please pray for me, too.'

Then Mother Luigi ushered us back to the novitiate.

Most of the novices were Kachins who spoke little English. The three Anglo-Indian ones had already taken their temporary vows and, at mealtimes, they sat at the same table as the professed nuns. I longed to speak to them, but any contact between nuns and novices on a social level was forbidden. A few days after they had professed their vows, the novices returned to their mission stations, taking all vestiges of fun and gaiety with them.

On Sundays we attended Mass at the cathedral. The Sacred Heart Cathedral of Toungoo lay near the centre of the town within a stone's throw of St. Joseph's Convent. Looking neither to the left nor the right, we walked to Mass in pairs, under the strict eye of the novice mistress. We genuflected before the Altar and entered the pews indicated by her. The high stained-glass windows depicted scenes from the Bible and reminded me of the cathedral in Mandalay. The occasional cough from the congregation, the perfume from the women and the cries of babies distracted my prayers, but the short walk to the cathedral was the only exercise permitted to us, and one of the rare occasions I was able to go outdoors.

When our canonical year came to a close, Sister Luigi said, 'The senior nuns feel you're not yet ready to take your vows, so you are to remain here for another year.'

Never had I been so wounded, so humiliated. My mind a maze of confusion, a lump arose to my throat. After obeying the rules, and abstaining from desserts as a sacrifice, *I had been turned down*. I made no protest however, realising I'd failed to subdue my inner feelings. Inwardly I rebelled against Mother Luigi, even though obeying outwardly. This indicated pride, and perhaps that is what the nuns had seen in me. Whatever the reason, the enforced postponement, the ultimate humiliation, crushed me.

In spite of my feelings, the thought of leaving the convent never entered my mind. I loved the silence and the prayer. The words, *Taste and see that the Lord is sweet*, still had a depth of meaning.

Rosie made her first vows for a year. Now known as Sister Rose, she was transferred to Taunggyi in the Shan States to commence her life away from the Mother House. It humbled me, but at the same time, I was glad we'd finally parted.

The nuns kept me in the novitiate with a new batch of novices for another year.

Barely had a few months elapsed, when a chronic cough developed because stress had weakened me and brought on a wheat allergy. Not used to eating the type of food served to the indigenous novices, Rosie and I had been given the same dishes as the Italian nuns, who had pasta dishes. Now, the stress of having attempted to suppress my feelings, weakened my body and brought on a wheat allergy. I coughed during the day and also in bed at nights. It wore me down, making me lean and gaunt.

We weren't allowed to look at ourselves in a mirror and there were none in the convent, but I sometimes gazed at my reflection in a window pane. My cheeks were pale and my eyes sunken with dark rings around them. I recalled having a chronic cough during the war. When we had beriberi from lack of vitamins, someone had suggested eating brown rice or whole wheat flour, so my father had made chapattis for us. We enjoyed it, and the swelling diminished slowly, but I developed a hacking cough, especially at nights. Mum used to rub my chest and back with her precious jar of Vicks Vapour Rub during those terrible times. When it ran out, Dad had bought blocks of camphor and Mum placed them in a bowl of cooking oil and left them in the sun until the camphor melted. She had then used the oil to rub my chest.

Now Mum wasn't here to care for me. The Mother Superior told me to take a sip of water whenever the bouts of coughing became uncontrollable. It helped a bit, and, apart from my cough, the year at the novitiate was rich and profound. Mother Luke, the nurse whom I'd met on my arrival at the convent, brought me some vitamin tablets. She shook her head and only said, 'Nervosa!'

Later on, when I studied Italian at the university, I realised it translated to 'Nerves!'

The year passed peacefully. The music teacher offered lessons on the organ to help me relax. My thoughts flew to my mother, who frequently sang while working, and to Bertie, who sang and played the guitar. My sister Rose also used to sing all day long. *Did little Winston enjoy singing too?*

Aware that my reflections had strayed from God, I wrenched my mind back and prayed for my family, finding solace in prayer and music. I floated on a cloud of ecstasy as winter passed and summer came and went. I prepared for the final phase before taking my vows.

Chapter 14

Lashio

Three years after entering the convent at Toungoo, in the winter of 1960, I was sent to a mission station. Life as a missionary among the newly converted hill tribes awaited me. This was my Apostolic year, but we referred to it as our Trial year as it tested our moral fibre. If we persevered, we were allowed to take our first vows.

'You'll be the youngest member of the community,' my novice mistress said before I left. 'Be guided by your Mother Superior and obey her in all things. Don't forget to be faithful to the rules you've been taught here.'

I resolved to serve the Lord to the best of my ability, and departed for Lashio, some one thousand metres above sea level on the Shan Plateau. A senior nun accompanied me. We boarded the train from Toungoo and on our arrival, took a pony cart from the station. On the way, I passed several bungalows and beautiful English-style country gardens. The trimmed hedges and blooms reminded me of long-ago days playing in the university gardens with my brothers and cousins.

The Guardian Angels' Convent was a U-shaped two-storey brick building. One wing housed the nuns' quarters; the other contained the Boarding House. The day school occupied the main section. In the foreground stood a large statue of an angel, ever-watchful over the convent and its occupants.

I joined a small community of four nuns—Mother Lena the

Mother Superior, two nuns and Sister Lucia, a novice in the final year of her triennial vows. Mother Lena was a charming young Italian nun of noble descent.

One of the other nuns, Mother Rosa, had a beautiful voice and wonderful sense of humour. I took an instant liking to her. 'My father discovered a huge rock of the finest jade, and made a fortune. He sent me to a boarding school at Maymyo, with the money he'd made. When I'd completed my studies there, I went to a Teachers' Training College before joining the congregation.'

Delighted to have a companion who spoke English so well, I grinned.

The grounds covered several acres of lawn, flower beds and playing fields for the students. We were allowed to walk in our own secluded area of the garden. I revelled in the sweet perfume of the flowers and the twittering of the birds. At sunset, myriads of mynas and parakeets settled on the treetops, their cacophony echoing back from the surrounding hills. As the evening mists descended, a grey shroud enveloped the trees. The beauty of creation drew me closer to God.

Not long after my arrival at Lashio, Mother Lena appointed me sacristan. Sister Lucia taught me everything before leaving to work in the kitchen. A sacristan's duties entailed looking after the tiny chapel, preparing the Altar for Mass every morning, and answering the responses of the priest at Mass. No task could have given me more joy than keeping the Chapel immaculate and polishing the huge brass and silver candlesticks. It was easy to serve the Lord in such a place. Nuns who work with the poor and the sick are called to a sterner test.

The linen was stored in long chests with deep drawers. In the mornings, I laid out the vestments and sacred vessels for Mass and put them away after the service. The vestments were embroidered with silk, and coloured red, white, green, gold, violet and black. Each colour represented the different seasons of the liturgical year. The changing hues of the vestments from the purple of Lent through the white and gold of Easter to the rose violet of

Advent, told of the passing year. What greater pleasure than being close to the Altar when love enveloped my heart?

Unlike the humidity of Rangoon or the hot, dry, dust of Mandalay the climate of Lashio was cool and refreshing in summer and cold in winter. I lingered in the garden when picking flowers to decorate the Altar. Their fragrance filled the atmosphere. My heart overflowed with happiness. Life was heaven on earth. No trace of the cough remained. *If this was a Trial Year, then life in the missions must be less austere than life in the Mother House.*

The twelve months at Lashio was the happiest time during my convent life. Besides looking after the Chapel, I had a class of junior students to teach. Some of the pupils stood head and shoulders above me. One of the boys, Mark, was far taller than the rest. An excellent student, he carried my books to and from the classroom and cleaned the blackboard.

I also had to supervise the students during the lunch hour. One day, Mark passed by. 'Good afternoon, Sister,' he called out.

I responded with my usual smile.

At that moment, Mother Lena happened to pass. 'Who's that?' Her normally sweet voice sounded like a hiss.

My eyes opened wide. 'My student, Mother.'

That question set me wondering whether I thought of Mark other than as a favourite student. I debated uneasily with my conscience, and confessed my doubts to the priest in the confessional. Obviously he didn't think it serious, because he didn't reprimand me or impose a large penance.

When the boarders returned home, during the April holidays, our little community of nuns had time to relax without the constant chatter of the girls. An unusual thing happened one day.

Mother Rosa paused to speak to me as I gathered the washing off the line. 'Did you know that Naga head hunters live in the hills around Lashio?'

The warm languid day induced a sensation of euphoria in me as I fumbled to reach the pegs. 'Do they?'

'Yes. They cut off their enemies' heads and shrink them. Then they hang the victims' heads around their huts.'

'Oh.' My exclamation was more like a breath to warm my fingers on a frosty morning, than the 'O' of an owl.

'The Nagas believe that human heads are a sign of a hunter's prowess. The shrunken skulls are supposed to appease the spirits and bring in a rich harvest of rice.'

I took another article of clothing off the clothes line, trying to keep my hands from trembling. 'I didn't realise they held such gruesome rites.'

'They live in dense jungles up in the mountains where civilised people rarely go.'

In the past three years within the novitiate, I'd never been allowed to have a friend or to speak freely. Now, a professed nun is speaking to me.

As we went in with the washing, I relaxed. *I haven't broken any Rules. Mother Rosa is a nun of many years standing, so this must be the accepted behaviour in mission stations.*

'In winter if the crop fails,' she continued, 'famine breaks out in the hills... Then better watch out... The head hunters come to Lashio and kidnap children for ...'

With eyes widened, I stopped folding the clothes I'd taken from the line and gave her my full attention. *Is this story something like the ones Bertie would spin to me, exaggerating the horror and describing everything in minute detail?*

'You're joking!'

She turned, giving me a dramatic bow. 'It's true. Cross my heart. Just before the war, about 1939 or so, government officials came to Lashio on a tour. A Sikh doctor accompanied them in case they fell ill with malaria or dengue fever. One day, the Nagas saw him washing his long hair and beard...'

I conjured up a vision of total horror in my mind. 'Oh. No.'

Mother Rosa ignored my interruption. 'They believed his head would bring blessings to their village and offered a reward of three hundred rupees for it.'

'That's a lot of money. Did the Nagas kill him?'

'No. The authorities came to hear of it and whisked him away to safety.'

Forgetting all about the clothes that lay in a pile on the carpet, I slid into a chair and begged for more stories.

Obviously pleased with such a willing audience, Mother Rosa settled back in her seat and told me of her adventures in the hills. 'We carried on our missionary work and travelled on mules, when visiting our flock in remote areas during the Japanese occupation. We tried to avoid Japanese patrols, but one day the Kachin look-out informed us that a Japanese patrol was heading to the village. I threw up my hands in despair. Our loyal Kachins told us not to be afraid and led us towards a vertical rock face deep within the jungle. On reaching the base of the bluff, a gigantic mass rose before us, forbidding further progress. Its summit remained hidden amongst the tree tops and looked like a mountain.'

'What did you do?'

'I prayed for help. Suddenly, a rope ladder snaked down the mountain and we clambered up.'

'That was a miracle! Did you hide in the trees?'

She chuckled. 'Once up the ladder, I found myself on a well-hidden plateau where the Kachins withdrew to hide from their enemies. The Kachins are experts in guerrilla warfare, and use their cunning to foil the enemy and attack them. Your uncle, Father George, was an army chaplain in the American and Kachin forces during the re-taking of northern Burma by the Allies.'

'Yes. He told me. He said he always slept with a gun in his sleeping bag, and was constantly on the alert.'

Thrilled by tales of adventure, my heart beat rapidly. I'd been confined to the novitiate for so long and had not been allowed to talk of my pre-convent days, or of *worldly* matters. Now, I abandoned myself to the sheer joy of the moment. Blissfully oblivious of the passing of time, I waited for more stories.

A contented smile on her face, Mother Rosa continued, 'Shans like a good joke and often play tricks on people. A girl once gave me a lovely bunch of flowers. I placed them in a vase and carried on teaching. Within a few minutes, overcome by drowsiness, I couldn't concentrate any longer. After setting my pupils some work I left, intending to lie down in my room. Their fits of giggling, followed me down the corridor.'

'Were you ill?'

'No. I just wanted to sleep and drift away without a care in the world, and didn't mind leaving my students unattended. It was so unusual.' She paused for dramatic effect. 'The next day, the girl confessed that she'd brought in some opium poppies from her father's garden.' Mother Rosa paused. 'The poppies had made me sleepy. Youngsters experiment with the drug and attempt to smuggle it into the boarding school, but we always supervise them at study or play. Even at night a sister occupies a corner of the girls' dormitory. Her bed is curtained off from the students and she remains alert to the least sound among them.'

Leaning back comfortably in the cane chair, she laced her fingers together. 'The Shan chieftains own rich ruby, silver and jade mines, and spare no money for the education of their children. Olive, whose father was a chieftain, led a colourful career after completing her studies here. Years later, she became a chief on her father's death and commanded a private army of about a thousand men. She established a lucrative trade in opium and smuggled truckloads of it to Thailand. Olive was finally caught. She languished for years in the notorious Insein Goal near Rangoon.'

'Was she imprisoned for life?' I asked.

Mother Rosa shook her head. 'At the termination of her imprisonment, she gave up her dangerous lifestyle and opened a Chinese restaurant in Rangoon.'

I leaned forward, eager for more. 'Did you know her?'

'No, but a nun passed on the story to me later on.'

Immersed in her tales, I failed to hear footsteps approaching. Mother Rosa seemed about to embark upon another adventure, when Mother Lena strode into the room. She gave one glance at the clothes piled upon the carpet, looked sternly at my companion, and left in silence.

The unspoken rebuke was sufficient to remind Mother Rosa of the rigid rules. 'Well. Must get back to work.' She lifted herself slowly from her chair.

I read the reluctance in her eyes.

Yet she never again indulged in any more stories, or sat down for a quiet chat. I guess she'd been reprimanded for her *tête-à-tête* with me.

The novice-mistress had told me the only conversation allowed was inner dialogue with Jesus. I should have admitted my fault to the Mother Superior but I'd enjoyed myself and had no regrets.

Neither did I confess my sin of disobedience to my confessor.

Chapter 15

Farewell to Bertie

Towards the end of my year at Lashio, Bertie wrote that he would be leaving for England. There were no prospects for him in Burma. Rose had now completed her studies, he said, and having fulfilled his duty towards his family, he now felt free to leave. He concluded his letter by saying he'd be driving up to see me before departing.

It was no surprise that Bertie had decided to quit Burma. After its independence in 1948, several Anglo-Indian families had migrated overseas to countries like England, the United States, Canada or Australia. Those who remained had taken out Burmese citizenship in the hope of continuing to work in government departments. But they had also clung to their British passports in case things got too hot in Burma. When a law proclaiming Burmese as the official language of the country was passed, the positions of Anglo-Indians in Burma remained uncertain, as only a few of them could read or write in Burmese.

My Mother Superior gave me permission to spend the day with my brother except during prayer and meal times. Thrilled at the thought of seeing him after so long, I barely slept that night. When Bertie arrived, we talked for hours, catching up on all the years, losing ourselves in the happiness of childhood bonds renewed.

Bertie told me he'd been engaged to an Anglo-Indian girl named Ann. 'We later quarrelled and broke off our engagement.'

'What are your plans?'

'Well, seeing that the political situation is rapidly deteriorating, I aim to get out of here as soon as possible.'

'But Mum told me that Uncle George had found you a good position at the Chauk oil fields in his parish. Must you leave?'

Bertie nodded. 'We're living under a military dictatorship that's so corrupt. Remember how rich Burma was in rubies, rice and teak? Now the country is bankrupt. The rate of pay is falling fast and the price of commodities is increasing.'

My voice dropped to a whisper. 'What'll you do in the UK?'

'Nursing. I've already done four years at Medical College and should get many exemptions. England is short of nurses.'

'I hope you'll be all right.' My heart ached for Bertie who'd left medical school when he was so close to being a doctor.

'Once I've settled in, I'll try to get Mum and the two younger ones to England as soon as I can.'

I placed my hand upon Bertie's. 'You always took care of Mum and the rest of us. You helped us all escape from our father and paid for Rose's boarding school fees. Now you're going to help the family leave Burma.' I paused, thinking of the past. 'What about Winston?'

'Winston. He loves music and is learning to play the guitar.'

'Yes. Just like you. I've seen him only twice since leaving home. Mum says he's full of fun and mischief. How is everyone? Mum looks the same, but hasn't Rose grown?'

'She's good-looking and well aware of it. A proper little flirt. Mum's still teaching at St. Peter's.' Bertie gazed at me, and then glanced up at the sky, watching the clouds scurrying past. With his eyes fixed on a particular cloud, he blurted out, 'Dad's been to Mandalay and seen Mum and the children.'

Like a submarine diving into the ocean and plunging deeper and deeper, to escape an enemy ship, my panic rose. *My family is in danger!*

'Mum refused to meet him without the nuns being present. Sister Martha accompanied her to the visiting room.'

'Poor Mum.'

'He asked her to return with him, and when Mum shook her head, he took her hand and solemnly divorced her, Muslim-style. Muslims have three forms of separation. In the absolute form of divorce, the words, *I divorce you*, are said three times. He chose the absolute form and Mum is now entirely free from him.'

'Well. Hope he'll leave us in peace.'

Bertie, with his forgiving nature, probably wondered how a novice, who'd consecrated her life to God, could not have the heart to forgive. But my father had abused me and it was difficult to pardon him.

'Dad gave Winston a little gift before he left,' Bertie continued, 'then he went up to Maymyo and visited Rose. She was supervised by the nuns, so he didn't dare entice her away. He gave her a pair of red shoes and a watch for her 13th birthday.'

Worry for my family clutched at my heart. 'That must have happened when Mum still lived in the Old Home run by the convent.'

'Yes. After the divorce, he took a *de facto* wife.'

My heart leaped. *Then Mum has nothing to fear from him any longer! So many things had happened in 1954 in quick succession. Little Trevor had died in March. A few months later, Uncle Pat had drowned and I had left for Myitkyina to join the Columban nuns! After I'd left, my father had visited Mum and his two youngest children. What a traumatic year it must have been for Mum, and yet she had told me nothing of his visit to spare me the worry.*

A choking sensation seized me. *Within a few minutes, my brother will be leaving me for ever.* I had steeled myself to accept the parting with composure, but the knowledge the moment was upon me drained me momentarily of strength. Swallowing hard, I recalled the songs he used to sing in the fifties: *Just Walking in the Rain, Marianne,* and *Rose, Rose, I love you.*

'There's a new song you must hear before I leave.' It was as if he'd read my thoughts. Then he sang *Put Your Head on My Shoulder.*

Sobs rose to my throat but I choked them back. As Bertie drove away, the trees seemed to close up behind him in the darkness.

That night the day's events whirled around my mind. My head throbbed with dread of the unknown and forebodings of the future. *Will Bertie have the opportunity to continue his studies in England? Will the rest of my family be able to join him before they are caught up in the maelstrom here?* I'd miss Bertie's cheerful face, but I had already given up my family for God. I was supposed to forget everyone, except in prayer, and only have thoughts of God.

I prayed for my family, willing to give up my life in return for their freedom. Despite this, my memory lingered on like faint traces of perfume, floating to the surface of my mind, enticing me towards life outside the convent. Nevertheless, each day, I took up the challenge of sacrificing my desires; content in doing God's will.

***

In July that year, Bertie bid farewell to Mum and Winston at Mandalay and drove down to Rangoon. He sailed for the UK on August 11 and wrote to me when the ship docked at Colombo. He said he was enjoying the sea voyage, but that he missed all of us.

I understood exactly what he felt. I enjoyed religious life but missed my family, especially little Winston.

***

The sixties became years of agony and tragic loss. In 1962, General Ne Win staged a coup. Soon people were arrested for speaking out against the army, and were never heard of again. In July, student leaders of the University of Rangoon condemned the military coup and called for a return of democracy. In retaliation, troops shot and killed dozens of students, set dynamite to the Students' Union Hall and shut down the campus.

***

On St. Columban's day in 1963, Sister Ita and Sister Andrew were caught in a skirmish between Kachin and Burmese troops. The nuns were nearly killed in the crossfire. Father Walsh, a hero of World War II and former chaplain to Merrill's Marauders, a group of American guerrillas, had been driving the nuns in his jeep. God spared his life that day but destiny caught up with him the following year.

Kachin villagers found his body lying in a shallow grave, his rosary beads under his face. Blood trickled from two bullet wounds in his head and one in his chest.

***

I was fortunate not to have been in Myitkyina with the Columban nuns during the sixties. Sheltered from the news of the outside world, I was unaware of the full implications of the growing tension within Burma until Bertie visited me.

Slowly, my eyes opened to the situation around me. *Civil war raged not far from us.* Once, during the monthly retreat—a day of prayer and silence I always looked forward to—the priest gave a sermon about martyrdom. Willing to shed my last drop of blood for Christ, I listened intently.

'Danger surrounds you,' the priest said. 'Nuns who live near the fighting zones are in jeopardy when weary and blood-stained soldiers from both sides arrive at their doors to have their wounds dressed. In convents like Africa, nuns are also at risk of rape, a fate worse than death.' He lowered his eyes but his voice rose. 'Remember that as long as there is no consent on your part, you remain guiltless of any sin should such a disaster ever occur.'

My heart sickened. I had dedicated my virginity to God. *Had I made this sacrifice only to lose it? God, who had taken such good care of me until now, would surely protect me from evil.* Fearful thoughts took hold of my mind, interspersed by uneasy slumber and indescribable anxiety. As time passed, my work in the chapel and at school dissipated my fears. The weeks glided by and my year away from the mother house at Toungoo drew to a close. I'd tasted the true life of a missionary.

Chapter 16

Back in the Novitiate

As my Trial Year in Lashio drew to a close, the Mother Superior called me to her office. I hurried after her, wondering whether she was going to reprimand me.

She beckoned me to a chair and went straight to the point. 'Why don't you speak to Sister Lucia?'

I'd thought she was going to tell me off for chatting to Mother Rosa and must have showed my surprise. 'Sister Lucia is never at recreation with us. She's always busy working in the kitchen.'

Mother Lena nodded. 'Well, Sister Lucia is to take her final vows and you are to accompany her to Toungoo, where you'll remain until you take your first vows.'

The senior novice was a shy girl from the Kachin hills, who had been assigned kitchen duties. I often wondered how she felt when she had been transferred from Chapel duties and delegated to working in the kitchen. She worked so hard and rarely spent our daily one hour of free time with us. *Did she have rebellious feelings?*

As the time for taking her profession approached, the novice was allowed to join the rest of the community after dinner. On the evening before our departure, she talked of her experience at a remote hill-station. 'One day a villager staggered up to the convent covered in blood. A bear had mauled him while he was hunting it. Sister Angela sewed him up and sent him to the infirmary.'

'Hope the poor beast got away.'

The novice's lips tightened and her eyes narrowed as though in pain. She'd been brought up in the hills, and knew it was the man's living. 'When he recovered from his wounds he captured the bear and sold it to some Chinese merchants. They use its bile as medicine. The money pays for food to feed his family.'

I'd known of the cruel methods used to extract bile from caged animals, and must have shown my disapproval. Conversation flagged. I beat my brains for something cheerful to say, but could think of nothing.

The following day after breakfast, we took the train and travelled all the way to Toungoo in silence.

***

Once back in the novitiate, Mother Luigi said, 'You are now a senior novice. You must sit with the professed nuns in the refectory and have your meals with them.'

Most of the nuns were elderly Italian nuns who'd served God in the mission stations and had returned to spend their last days in the Mother House. Some taught in the school but the old and feeble ones occupied their days in prayer. They were pointed out to us as a living example of our holy rules. I was a bit nervous to sit at their table but looked forward to more appetising food as the meals were made to please their failing appetites. I soon learned to love Italian cuisine, and particularly enjoyed the risotto dishes, beef ravioli with fresh vegetables and the dessert of tiramisu, which we received on feast days.

The year passed peacefully except for an incident that disturbed the serenity of the convent. One night, during the Grand Silence, a novice screamed and woke us from our sleep.

'A man was standing beside my bed. He took off when I screamed.'

The novices picked up any weapon available—brooms, sticks, spades and shovels, and searched for the intruder. We glided around silently like spectres in our white nightdresses, clutching our weapons and searching the passageways and cupboards.

After some time, the Novice Mistress hurried us back to bed, not once reprimanding us for speaking during the Grand Silence.

Frightened whisperings among the novices continued until the early hours of the morning, when everyone settled down.

After that unforgettable night, the priest's warning at Lashio about rape came back to haunt my mind. I remained in fear, unable to still my trembling. Whenever alone before the Blessed Sacrament at nights, I knelt and prayed but started at the slightest sound. The chapel was isolated from the rest of the Convent. Toungoo has a warm climate and we had no air-conditioning or fans to keep the place cool, so the door and windows were left open to let in fresh air. *Our convent is surrounded by a high brick wall that had kept out intruders under British rule and even during Japanese occupation of Burma. Now times are changing and a wall is no deterrent to a thief or rapist. If someone enters and attempts to molest me, none of the nuns will hear my screams for help!*

Unable to concentrate on my prayers, I glanced around every now and then to check whether an intruder had entered the chapel. I dared not confide in my novice mistress, thinking she would only tell me to have more faith in the Lord.

Like most semi-contemplative orders, the Sisters of Reparation recited excerpts from the Divine Office. At nine in the mornings, we recited the Church's Morning Prayer, asking for the Lord's blessings on the new day. We also said Prime at 2 pm and Vespers at 5 pm. On school days, I was absent for the 9 am and 2 pm office recitals, and envied the novices who attended all three recitals. They scarcely spoke English, but learned to say the Divine Office, their loud young voices overpowering those of the elderly Italian nuns. Most of them were fervent converts from the hills. The novice mistress drilled them like an army sergeant and somehow, she succeeded in instilling in them the importance of obeying the rules and regulations.

One of the novices had an exceptionally long neck, and reminded me of a giraffe I'd seen at the Rangoon zoo. Fascinated by its extraordinary length, my eyes were frequently drawn to her slender throat.

The novice mistress called me aside one day. 'Have you forgotten to practise custody of the eyes in just one short year away from the novitiate?' she admonished. 'Don't forget that what you learn here is a life-long commitment. The girl you stare at is a member of the Palaung hill-tribe. Their custom is to put rings around their daughters' necks because they think it adds to their beauty.'

I'd seen Palaungs when my family had spent our annual holiday at Kalaw and thought of my two brothers, Rupert and Bertie walking ahead with my father. June and I had lingered behind with Mum, stopping now and then to pick raspberries or collect pine cones.

I stood silently before the Novice Mistress. To make excuses or speak of the past was forbidden.

'She is one of the more fortunate ones and still has the use of her neck muscles,' Mother Luigi continued. 'The Palaungs converted to Christianity and the cruel custom stopped. Some of the girls couldn't hold up their heads after the rings were removed because the muscles had wasted away. They flopped sideways.'

My eyes widened. *It would have been more merciful to have replaced the rings for those girls.*

Mother Luigi allowed me more spare time than the junior novices. During school vacations, I had time off for a siesta after lunch, was allowed to practise on the organ and continue with my music lessons. The convent library was at my disposal and I indulged in reading and learning about the lives of saints. My favourite book was *The man who got even with God* by M Raymond, the true story of a short-tempered youth who entered a Trappist monastery and nearly killed a fellow monk in a rage. Eventually the young monk attained sainthood through prayer and self-control.

An all-pervading peace, together with an ineffable sense of joy at being one with God, reigned within me as I tried hard to overcome my impatience and prepare myself for the next major step in convent life. Confident of dedicating my entire life to the Lord, I looked forward to taking my temporary vows for a year.

***

A month before my profession, the Mother Superior sent me to recuperate in a convent at Kutkai, in the remote Kachin hills, not far from Tanghpre where Bertie had worked. An elderly nun accompanied me as we walked to the bus station. Natives squatted cross-legged, squirting streams of betel juice from their stained lips.

Fascinated by the scarlet-stained sidewalks, I recalled the time a woman spat on the sidewalk in Rangoon. Turning to my mother, I'd exclaimed, 'Look, Mummy! She's hurt her mouth and is bleeding terribly.'

My mother chuckled and then explained the native habit of chewing betel nut. 'They mix the cracked nut with lime paste and spices, wrap it in a leaf and chew it for hours. It has a sedative effect and stains their lips and teeth a bright red.'

I wrenched back my thoughts to my present surroundings. A lake dotted with islands hid a history of kings stretching back over one hundred and fifty years. Gazing at the peaceful scene, I followed the elderly nun's quickening steps and boarded the bus. Passengers crammed their bundles and baskets in luggage racks or on the floor near their seats.

My companion picked her way along the aisle. I followed, and took a seat beside her. Within minutes, several explosions rocked the vehicle. I rose, looking around for shelter, imagining an attack by rebels.

The nun gently tugged at my sleeve. 'Don't worry. The bus backfired while trying to start.'

The engine coughed out fumes in a series of explosions. After a few minutes it shuddered into life, jerked forward and toiled its way up the mountains. Despite the cramped conditions, the journey was most enjoyable. The wind sang in the trees and birds circled against the blue sky. Wildflowers grew everywhere. The heavy scent of meadowsweet mingled with the delicate perfume of dog roses. The Sittang River, made infamous during World War II with the death of thousands of Allied troops, flowed past. The mountains loomed nearer and soon we left the green foothills behind. The fresh, bracing air of the hills exhilarated me.

A steep and winding road brought us to the convent gates, where the ancient bus discharged us. The driver asked us to point out our luggage and flung them down. We picked up our things and trudged uphill towards the building.

Mother Olga, the Mother Superior, was busy but sent two young nuns to show us our rooms. After our evening meal, she welcomed us and took me to her garden. She'd learned farming from her parents and had done marvels with her vegetables. 'Plants sowed during the waning moon are stunted and unhealthy. Those planted at the waxing phase grow tall and strong.'

I loved gardening, and, fascinated by her method of planting, treasured her words, not realising I'd use the same system, years later.

Most villages had a raised hut placed over a hole in the ground—a seething, bubbling ferment infested by maggots and flies. They emitted a disgusting odour. The toilet at Kutkai, however, was unlike any others. Here it was built over the earth without a pit or pail to hold the faeces, yet it remained clean and odourless. During my first visit to the toilet, pigs tore at each other over the stools. Some alighted on a pig's ear, and another lunged forward, taking a piece of its companion's ear with the faeces. The pig's squeal must have reached every corner of the convent.

Filled with revulsion at seeing them feed on my droppings, I avoided eating pork whenever possible.

As the students were on holiday, the Mother Superior allowed me to roam in the convent grounds. 'You're here to regain your health, so you're to do nothing but rest and refresh yourself. You may only join the community at meals and prayers.'

The novelty of leisure was similar to a caress and I received it gratefully. While indulging in the pure mountain air, my thoughts floated back to walks in the village with my sister Rose, just before the war ended. She was a young woman now, and though not aware of it at the time, she'd one day teach at Namtu, a convent not far from Kutkai.

I wandered down the hill to a little stream that flowed through the grounds and gazed at it, longing to remove my shoes and paddle in the water.

When the desire persisted, I confided my deep yearning to Mother Olga.

To my surprise, she said, 'It's not likely you'll be seen by anyone. Go ahead and have a swim during recreation.'

Clad only in my nightgown, with a towel draped around my shoulders, I threaded my way towards the water. The star-studded sky was calm and beautiful. The moon created a pathway of light on the stream. The silver skein sliding silently over the water brought back memories of swimming in the Kokine Lakes with my family. My heart beat fast in anticipation of immersing myself in the water. I stepped gingerly in, and lay there, stimulated by the cold current. The soft lapping of the waves caressed my body and aroused a sense of exquisite delight—the only sensual pleasure I'd indulged in since entering the novitiate.

The days passed swiftly. My health improved and the coughing subsided as the time for me to leave those healthy surroundings drew nearer. The prospect of living here after taking my vows was not an unpleasant one— even though it was so remote from civilisation.

On the evening before my departure, the convivial Kachin nuns invited me to taste some of their local wine. Visions of my alcoholic father had kept me from indulging in wine or spirits and I scarcely ever touched it. A glass of port or sherry on Christmas and New Year's Day was my limit. Not wanting to offend the nuns, however, I threw back my head and drained the contents. My body glowed with warmth. My pulse raced. I became light-headed and shouted with joy as the heat rose to my face.

The nuns laughed. 'You're drunk.'

My voice rose. 'I'm *not* drunk.'

The bell sounded for night prayers and everyone fell silent. I staggered to chapel behind the others. The flowers on the altar danced merrily and the candles winked at me in delight. Carried away with a strange sensation, I flung away all restraint and talked loudly. Everyone smiled at me.

After prayers, I reeled back to my room, threw myself upon the bed and slept like a drugged person the whole night.

The next day I awoke late, my head pounding. The slightest sound magnified itself a hundredfold. The clanging of bells jarred on my nerves. I rose from bed, sick in the stomach and skipped breakfast without permission.

Overcome by remorse, and thoroughly ashamed of myself, I apologised to Mother Olga before leaving for the novitiate, expecting to be given a severe reprimand and a heavy penance at the Mother House.

Mother Ester, a benevolent autocrat, smiled when I told her what had happened. To my surprise and delight, she invited Mum, Rose and young Winston for my profession—a major step in my religious life.

My family had first visited me barely a year after I'd left home. Now, three years later, at my Profession, young Winston had grown much taller, and he'd already made his First Communion. He had written to me a few times during my first two years in the novitiate, and I treasured his letters. I coaxed him to sing for me. My heart thrilled when he sang a few strains of *Hang down your head, Tom Dooley*.

As for Rose, gone was the thin, gangly sister I'd left and whose dresses I used to sew. She'd wanted us to dress alike. I'd been too embarrassed then, as people tended to stare, and I never liked to attract notice. Now an attractive young lady with tailor-made clothes had emerged like a butterfly from a silkworm.

Only then did I realise the full impact of the passage of time. In the novitiate, we had to cut ourselves off from the outside world. What solely mattered was the bell that rang to wake us each morning, to pray, go for meals, or retire for the night. It was the voice of God and told us what to do and when to do it. Time meant nothing. Only eternity mattered. Like a bolt of lightning, it hit me that I'd already lost count of months and years, and could not even remember the date I had entered the convent. So well had the nuns succeeded in eradicating the sense of time.

At my profession, I knelt at the Altar with ten other novices and received a white veil and silver ring with a crucifix on it as a token of my pledge. I hoped to wear a black veil and a gold ring, in three years' time. Now known as Sister Hazel, the sweetness of the Lord overwhelmed me. When my turn for the prayer vigil came, I draped myself from head to foot in a white silk cloak bordered with red. The white stood for purity and the red for martyrdom, signifying my willingness to shed my blood for Christ. I knelt on a *prie-dieu*, feeling very close to God during these precious moments. This hour enshrouded within the cloak enhanced my spirits. It was the most wonderful moment of the day. Throbbing with fervour, and gazing steadfastly at the Blessed Sacrament, I prayed for my family, my community and for sinners. But even then, it was difficult to forgive my father.

After my first vows, the nuns kept me to teach in Toungoo. Because the numbers of novices were increasing, Mother Josephine, whom I'd met when I was a postulant, was appointed an Assistant Novice Mistress. Now a fully professed nun, she helped run the novices, so I could speak freely to her without breaking any rules.

Tall and slim, a smile lurked in the corners of her mouth. Her open, honest countenance invited confidence. We became the best of friends. If only I'd known her earlier! She introduced me to her sisters. The elder was a matron in the Operating Theatre of Toungoo General Hospital, and the younger ones, Magda and Christine, were university students.

Mother Ester sent for me one day. 'All foreign missionaries will soon be expelled from Burma, and it is up to the indigenous nuns to carry on. Future mother-superiors should be fully qualified. It's no longer sufficient to have a teacher's diploma in order to be the principal of a school. A university degree is imperative, so you are to study towards a degree. We'll enrol you as an off-campus student.'

I wanted to devote my time to prayer, and disliked the thought of being a mother-superior someday. But I had no choice in the matter. The nuns enrolled me as an external student at the University of Rangoon. Magda, who'd done her Bachelor of Arts degree the previous year, passed on her lecture notes to me. Gratitude overwhelmed me, but I fought back the impulse to embrace her. Hugging was forbidden.

Although permitted to write to my family, Mother Luigi censored all my correspondence. At first I'd been horrified to know that my novice mistress read both incoming and outgoing letters. Mum's letters were filled with concern about Rose, who was now the most popular girl at every party. My sister also wrote to me of the wild parties she attended, describing dances like the Limbo Rock, and going to beer gardens with her friends.

The novice mistress warned me. 'Your sister will be the cause of your leaving the convent.'

I smiled and shook my head. *Nothing could make me leave my peaceful haven.*

Chapter 17

Home

Time passed. I thought of the long wait at the convent gates on my first day, the nun who greeted me and the silence of the place. The years spent in striving for perfection had no yardstick to measure time, and no worldly event to celebrate. No milestones such as birthdays, marriages, birth or death marked the passing of each day. Just stillness and God. The constant struggle within had been demanding but, in retrospect, the days had been a period of peace and joy.

In January each year, novices made their vows and professed nuns returned to the Mother House in Toungoo for their annual retreat. Those who were to take their final vows were allowed to visit their families prior to taking their vows. The short break gave them time to decide whether to return to the world or remain on forever in their chosen congregation. As a result of this, I was given permission to stop at home for a few days, on my way to St. Anne's Convent, Taunggyi. *What will it be like to live as a nun outside the seclusion of the novitiate? Has my family changed? Have I?*

***

I stepped down from the train and waved goodbye to the nun, who had accompanied me to Mandalay. She was proceeding to her own mission station further north.

Mum waited on the platform, her arms outstretched. Her face spoke volumes. Taking both my hands in hers, as if we were about to dance a reel together, she stood back speechless with pride, gazing at me. Then she hugged me. 'Let's go Hazel. I've hired a pony-cart.'

'Oh Mum. You're looking so well. I've missed you. We're supposed to leave everyone and everything in God's hands, but I worry over you.'

Mum caressed my silver crucifix-ring with her fingers.

I smiled. 'We kiss it whenever we make the Sign of the Cross, and renew our vows silently each time.'

We entered the pony-cart. The driver touched the scrawny pony with his stick, and it clomped along the streets. My eyes were on Mum until we stopped in front of the garden gate. She looked the same, but our home seemed different.

'You know Mum, so much has happened since leaving home. I don't quite remember the house we used to live in after hostilities. Thought it was red brick.'

'Just goes to show you're so engrossed in learning to be a nun that the world has ceased to exist.' She paused, then chuckled at her little joke. 'We've plastered the walls to hide the cracks. The house is painted white too.' She squeezed my hand. 'Come inside. I've a lot to tell you. Rose and Winston are waiting.'

'Are they still the same?'

Mum shook her head.

'Changed much?' Without pausing for a reply, I descended from the pony-cart, and held a hand out to help Mum.

A creeper wound itself up the trellised arch above the little wooden gate and a sparrow chirped. When Mandalay had been retaken by British forces, the front door of our house had been peppered by shrapnel. I climbed the stone steps and glanced up at the massive teak door, looking for the shrapnel scars. The holes had been blocked with a less expensive timber.

We entered the lounge room. The house felt warm and inviting, the radio played a lively tune and the aroma of cooking drifted towards me. Coming in from the dazzling sunlight, I saw nothing but a blur for a few seconds. When my vision cleared, Rose and Winston were sitting together on the settee. They rose to their feet and greeted me with a kiss. Rose flipped her hair back and Winston combed his with his fingers. I sensed their unease. *A nearly-professed nun, who had intruded into their lives, must seem strange to them. They had changed. They'd grown up.*

'What a lovely young lady you are, Rose.' I looked at her, then turned to Winston, who was in his shirtsleeves. 'You're quite a gentleman.' My hand went out, touching his biceps. 'You're taking weights.'

'Show Hazel your weights,' Mum said.

Winston cast a sidelong glance at Rose but did not stir.

Mum smiled. 'Do we call you Hazel?'

'Of course.'

Only Mum had not changed. She was still the same mother; her faith as firm as ever, her love even stronger with the passing of years. She excused herself and left. The clattering of plates in the dining room told me she was preparing the table for dinner. Rose, usually so talkative, moved her body in time to the music. Apart from the radio, silence filled the space between us.

Mum called: 'Dinner is ready.'

Steeped in the habit of prompt obedience, I immediately left what I was going to say unsaid. I walked down the hallway, past the three bedrooms and entered the dining room. A checked gingham tablecloth graced the table and a vase with fresh flowers stood in the centre. Mum pointed to my place and asked me to say Grace. I made a large Sign of the Cross and recited the blessing, remembering the times Mum had commenced our meals with a prayer. Rose and Winston stood with heads bowed, Mum said, 'Amen,' and we all sat down to dinner.

After several squints out of the corner of his eyes, Winston finally broke the uncomfortable silence. 'Well, what's it like being a nun?'

'Winston, stop teasing,' Mum said.

I started to giggle. Rose joined in, and soon we were all laughing until tears ran down our cheeks.

'I'm sure everyone wants to ask that question,' I said, once I'd stopped giggling. I described life within a convent, but neither Rose nor Winston could understand why anyone chose to live in such a manner.

'Where does it get one? What does it achieve?' Winston asked.

Convent life, a life I cherished, seemed pointless to them.

After dinner, Rose and Winston went off to do their own thing. Both were on holidays for the Christmas break, and had a lot of catching up to do with friends. Mum gave me all the latest news about the family. She unburdened her worries to me; things she couldn't put down in writing, especially as letters were censored.

'I worry over Rose.' She bit her lip.

'I thought boarding school would do her a world of good.'

Mum shook her head. 'The nuns trained her well, but she's turned out to be a little flirt. She attends so many parties and returns home late.'

'Has she been in trouble?'

'No. She used to come home at midnight, at first; now it's two or three o'clock in the mornings. I stay up praying for her every time she's out.'

'What are her friends like?'

'They're good Catholics, mostly from Cathedral Street. I know their parents. The ones I've met seem nice. Can't pin-point the problem.'

'Perhaps she's growing up and will settle down later.'

'You may be right, but your father's strict upbringing may have been better for her. I allow her too much freedom.'

'Poor Mum. All I can do is to pray for you.'

'Yes, Hazel. Please do. I go to Mass in the Cathedral every day, and pray for God's guidance.'

'He won't let you down.'

'Hazel, will you come to Mass with me, or join the St Joseph nuns in their Chapel?'

I gave her a hug. 'With you, of course.'

Mum smiled in delight.

I hesitated, then asked, 'Will you marry again, now that you're free?'

Mum shook her head. 'I'll dedicate my life to God and to my children.'

***

Warmth spread throughout my body as I knelt beside Mum in Church.

She had her favourite spot in the first row on the right side, near Our Lady's altar.

On the last day, I visited my old teachers at St. Joseph's Convent.

The few days at home soon came to an end. I enjoyed the brief space of rest and liberty in our dear home among my loved ones. My heart filled with sorrow when it was time for me to leave.

Mum, Rose and Winston took me to the station and saw me safely on the train. A nun waited in a carriage to accompany me to Taunggyi for my final year as a novice. There I was to experience life as a missionary nun once more.

A lump rose to my throat as I waved goodbye to my family forever. The distance between me and my two siblings seemed like a great chasm. Already we appeared to have grown apart.

Chapter 18

Taunggyi

Taunggyi means *Big Hill*. Cloaked in pines and nestled in the hills on the Shan Plateau, the town had been a respite from the summer heat for the British in pre-war days. Now, the only reminders of a bygone era were a cemetery overgrown by moss and vines, an avenue of cherry trees leading to a stone church and some cottages on the outskirts of town. Walking tracks wound their way to the summit. I longed to hike along the trails and wondered if the nuns sometimes went for walks on the hills.

A delightful garden, even lovelier than the one at Lashio, surrounded St Anne's Convent. Sister Rose had spent her first year from the Mother House here, and was now stationed seventy kilometres west, at Kalaw.

On my arrival at Taunggyi, Sister Louise-Clare greeted me warmly. I had previously met her at Toungoo, but never had the opportunity of speaking more than a few words to her. Tall, with a friendly smile and a face sprinkled with freckles that gave her a mischievous look, her eyes danced beneath a pair of heavy spectacles. Being the only young women amidst a convent of aged and ailing nuns, an unspoken bond grew between us. One of the nuns, Mother Mary Agnes, had been a teacher at St. Joseph's in Mandalay, and had taught Mum. Although frail and in poor health, she continued teaching. Mother Andrew, the mother-superior, was tall, thin and erect, with a lean, pale face. She lived on a Spartan diet. Always grave, she ruled the convent with a firm hand.

Sister Louise-Clare was in charge of the boarding school. We took turns to supervise the students' study and meals, and only met when relieving each other of our duties. It was something like the changing of the guard at Buckingham Palace. No conversation or words were exchanged. Just silence.

My bed stood in a corner of the girls' dormitory. Mother Andrew told me to meditate in my curtained-off area while the girls had a shower and dressed for school, instead of having my morning meditation in the chapel with the nuns. I could not join them in chapel for prayers either.

Meditation had always been difficult for me even in the peaceful precincts of the chapel, but now it became a time of rebellious thoughts and frustrations. Seated in a dormitory with sixty teenagers, contemplation was a sheer impossibility. Some girls lingered before a mirror, admiring themselves. Others stopped and talked to their friends. I had to hurry them along to shower and dress so that they'd be in time for dinner.

Unable to have my evening meal with the rest of the community, I dined alone after watching over the students at their dinner. I also had to sacrifice evening prayers with the other nuns, because of having to supervise the girls' study hour.

As a consequence of long hours spent with the boarders, my prayer-life suffered. All I did was watch over the girls. *Why had I joined a convent? Was it not to have time for prayer?* These questions burned into my soul.

I told the Mother-Superior about my difficulty in praying while supervising students. 'There's a strain on my inner-life, Mother.'

'You have God in your heart and should be able to pray anywhere. Your heart is your private Chapel.' Her look was stern. 'Sister Rose had the same duties when here, but never complained.'

My heart beat faster and a sound like rushing water filled my ears. All my old resentment flared up, leaving me seething with anger. *I'd turned to her for help but she has accused me of complaining! Is this what convent-life is? A mere grind from day to day with no time for contemplation in peaceful surroundings?* Immersed in my daily duties, I lost much of my enthusiasm for prayer. A wave of black despair swept over me.

Spring arrived, bringing delightful weather. Birds sang but my heart no longer filled with joy. Summer brought a flush of roses but my cheeks failed to bloom. The reds and golds of autumn lit neither the flame of faith nor the fire of joy in my heart. Winter filled me with a cold fear because the time for my final vows fast approached. The Mother Superior continued to keep me busy with the students.

A nun's life is dedicated to sacrifice. The only relaxation permitted is to talk among ourselves during the one-hour recreation period in the evening. In the novitiate, so many restrictions had been placed on our conversation. Besides, I had nothing in common with the novices, whose English was not fluent. It irked me to speak with someone who every now and then stumbled for the correct word. I preferred to pray in the Chapel alone with God. However, back at Toungoo, the novice mistress had rebuked me. 'Recreation is a rule like any other and you should not spend that time apart from your sisters. You are in a community and must live together in harmony, especially during recreation.'

Here, at Taunggyi, I barely had time even for that hour of relaxation with the nuns, as Sister Louise-Clare and I took turns supervising the students. I never had the opportunity of spending an hour of relaxation with the young nun, and found nothing to speak about with the elderly ones who engaged in small talk among themselves. Occasionally, they drew me into the conversation with a few choice remarks but I was not at ease and hardly ever spoke. Misery weighed me down like a ton of bricks.

Taunggyi is only a forty-five-minute drive by road from the picturesque Inle Lake, which was 1338 metres above sea-level. Known as 'the Venice of Asia', the lake has little islands of floating vegetation on which the inhabitants build their huts. There leg rowers ply their boats, standing like cranes on one limb, with the other tucked around an oar. Inle Lake was so close to our convent, but we were never given the opportunity to view this particular one of God's majestic creations.

Time dragged on. How true the adage, 'All work and no play makes Jack a dull boy.' My spare time was devoted to study—my only escape after daily chores. All I wanted now was to be alone with my books. In the mornings when the mists rose like a curtain, my soul remained shrouded in darkness. The dark face of the hills, visible in the distance, failed to fill my soul with joy, as in former times. At nights, the stars glittered like fragments of glass, tearing my heart to shreds. Still I struggled on, hoping the sun would shine on my soul again, illuminating it with the love of prayer once more.

***

A single incident stands out clearly during that long and tedious year. One night, Sister Louise-Clare approached me. 'I must speak to you urgently.'

She must have something important to communicate, as no one speaks during the Grand Silence. I recalled that the novice mistress had often pointed out Sister Louise-Clare as a model, saying, 'Imitate her.' *Am I about to be rebuked? But surely it is the Mother Superior's job to talk to me if I fail in my duties? Is it so vital that it cannot wait until morning?*

Two sepulchral figures clad only in our white nightgowns, we chose a quiet corner, and sat close to each other so the students wouldn't overhear. After a few tense moments, Sister Louise-Clare blurted out, 'I'm leaving tonight.'

'Are you being transferred?'

'No. I'm leaving the convent.'

My voice trembled. 'But you've taken your final vows. Did you get a dispensation from the Pope?'

'It'll take too long. I'll be joining my parents who have migrated to England and will marry as soon as the Pope has dispensed me from my vows.' After chatting of her future plans, Louise-Clare said, 'Will you marry if you ever return to the world?'

'I've no intention of leaving the convent.' I was flabbergasted at the seemingly pointless question.

'What if you found you didn't fit in, and had to leave? Would you marry?' Louise-Clare insisted.

My fingers groped beneath my night-bonnet to scratch my head. 'Perhaps I would.'

Sister Louise-Clare rose to her feet. 'Promise me not to tell the nuns I spoke to you about my departure.'

I nodded.

'Goodbye. May God guide and bless you.' She kissed me on both cheeks, turned, and left me forever.

I lay awake for hours. For the first time I'd wilfully broken Grand Silence. However it upset me even more to know that Louise-Clare, a model nun, was breaking her vows. *If she did that, what hope was there for me to keep mine?* Self-doubt raised its ugly head. Dizzy with indecision, battling with the thoughts pressing upon me, fear crushed the breath out of my chest. An introvert, unlike those effervescent, extrovert characters like Louise-Clare, I rarely had a rapport with any of the nuns. *What if I'm not compatible to community life?* The thought of leaving *after* my final vows now oozed into my troubled consciousness like mud, weighing me down as I tossed and turned in bed. Part of me strove for perfection and the rest longed for satisfaction—like the dark side of the moon—the side never exposed to others. One day it could break away from its orbit. Escape from the force of gravity and reveal its hidden side.

The vows of Poverty, Chastity and Obedience controlled every minute of the day, every second of the night. The vow of Poverty didn't bother me. I'd never hankered for wealth or known want in pre-war days. We never went hungry in the convent. If the food was insipid, the meals were nourishing, and all our needs were catered for. All we had to do was ask. But the vow of Poverty did not merely mean giving up possessions. We also had to give up attachments to things like a favourite book a hot-water bottle or an afternoon siesta. An attachment to a job too was regarded as a fault. *Had I not been devoted to my task as sacristan at Lashio, to my afternoon siestas during vacations, the music lessons at the novitiate and my studies at the university?*

Obedience was not too difficult. *Spending endless hours with the boarders at the cost of sacrificing time for prayer was bothersome, but a novice's duties frequently change. Supervising the girls will not be a lifetime job. The older nuns are given much more time in the chapel. As the years pass, I hope to have more hours for prayer.*

But what about indifference to my reputation? How well did I accept humiliation? Admittedly, I had learned not to make excuses, but had I not rebelled inwardly and fumed with anger when slighted or put down? Did I not consider myself superior to the other novices and never confessed the fault?

Chastity, the most difficult of all, was unchanging and remained a lifelong commitment. I had repressed my sexuality by using the metal chain on my thigh and grown in spirituality by prayer and sacrifice. Although attracted to some members of the opposite sex before entering the convent, I'd chosen a life of celibacy. No one had forced me to enter the convent. Yet a physical restlessness within me still persisted. At times, it grew in intensity until it became a pain—an ache screaming out for satisfaction that swelled like a dam about to burst its banks.

Assailed by doubts, I questioned my vocation. *It will be better to leave now before I take my final vows,* I debated, sensing a loss of confidence in my own will power. *I'll be bound for life once I make my Perpetual Vows, and if life becomes too unbearable, I will have to apply to the ecclesiastical authorities for a dispensation from Rome. I must act before it is too late.* Thoughts swirled around my head, making sleep impossible. The seconds ticked away until the clock struck two.

Finally, sleep brought relief to the tumult of my mind, but even then I slept restlessly with a sense of fever in my veins.

The next morning Sister Louise-Clare was absent from breakfast. No one mentioned her.

'Is she ill?' I asked, wondering whether they'd tell me the truth.

Someone mumbled a half-audible reply.

A few days later, one of the nuns told me that Sister Louise-Clare had gone to visit her sick parents.

I hated deceit of any form, and longed to return to the Mother House. I did not accuse myself of having spoken during Grand Silence, thus adding the sin of omission to my sin of disobedience to the Rule.

It was impossible to shake off the depression. The future remained enveloped in an impenetrable haze. The dreariness of the monsoons under weeping skies was in tune with my feelings. A chilly wind swept around the cold convent with violence and a blast of icy wind hit me like a slap in the face. *What is happening beyond the convent walls? I've spent years shut off from it. So many things must have occurred since then. Will I find things changed if I return to the world outside?*

Although unaware of world events, changes had been introduced into the Church, and more freedom given to religious nuns and brothers. It was for this reason that, just prior to being posted out to St. Anne's, I had been allowed to spend a few days at home with my family at Mandalay. The Church wanted to give me a last chance to change my mind, *but I had not wavered until now.*

Chapter 19

Disillusioned

At long last the day of departure from Taunggyi approached. A letter arrived, recalling me to the Mother House at Toungoo to make a ten-day retreat dedicated to prayer, sermons, silence and preparation for my final vows.

A senior nun from another convent accompanied me. I'd hoped my love of prayer would return once back in the novitiate, but my prayers were arid. The abyss of silence dismayed me. Usually ecstatic during retreats, now I thought solely of Louise-Clare and her broken vows. I only found comfort in music.

One day I was playing the organ in the music room when Mother Therese, a senior Anglo-Indian nun, spoke. 'How do you feel about your brother leaving Burma?'

'Feel about it?' I repeated, parrot-like.

'What will you do when your whole family leaves the country?'

'Jesus said to leave one's family and follow Him. I've done that already, and it should not matter whether they are in Mandalay or London.' I tilted my head to one side and pursed my lips. *Why does she ask so many questions, knowing I'm not allowed to speak to senior nuns?*

I had begun to doubt my own vocation ever since Louise-Clare left. Beneath my bonnet I had allowed my hair to grow in case I decided to do the same.

During our monthly *tête-à-tête* I told the Novice Mistress about my spiritual dryness, and revealed what I'd done.

'Trust in the Lord. He is testing your love and faith,' she said. 'Even saints experience the dark night of the soul at some time or the other. Show your faith by cutting your hair and crushing all doubts.'

Bound by the vow of obedience, I cut my hair, but remained restless and unresolved. Neither able to kneel nor sit still, I had a strong desire to pace up and down like a caged animal in a zoo.

As the ten-day retreat drew to a close, my dreams became troubling. In one, I was lying in bed with a man. A deep sense of satisfaction overwhelmed me while a voice said, *'This is what you will be missing forever.'* The words seared themselves on my brain. The same dream recurred for three nights in succession.

I went to confession and told the priest about my dreams.

'Did you dream of any particular man?' he asked.

'No. I didn't see his face, but I don't think I've ever seen him.'

The priest knew my vows would expire within a few days. 'Go to your Novice Mistress and tell her you have been advised to leave the convent. You've dedicated so many years of your life to Him, so God will bless you with a good husband.' He gave me absolution and a special blessing for my future life.

I've cut my hair in obedience to instructions, so I'll have to face the world with short hair in a country where most women have long flowing hair. I'll stand out like a sore thumb. I fisted my hands into a tight ball until my nails bit into my flesh. Then pain rose in my chest, and I broke out into a cold sweat.

I spoke to my Novice Mistress, telling her it would be far better for me to leave now, rather than after my final vows. I divulged the secret talk with Louise-Clare, which had been weighing upon my conscience.

Mother Luigi bit her lip. 'Wait here. I need to speak to our Mother Regional about this.'

My pulse quickened. *Will she try to persuade me to stay?*

A few minutes later, Mother Luigi returned. 'Mother Ester would like to see you.'

Mother Regional appeared downcast. She said nothing and only pointed to a seat opposite her. I anticipated a lecture.

Perhaps she was too disappointed in me to speak. She opened a safe that stood beside her desk, took out an envelope with my name on it, and returned my dowry of five hundred kyats. 'Canon Law states that the dowry paid by a nun at the time of her religious profession must be returned to her if she leaves the convent. Please sign for it.'

'May I keep my silver crucifix ring?'

She nodded, gave me her blessing and kissed me goodbye, her face unsmiling.

The next day dawned, still and humid. Mother Luigi told me to remain in the novitiate when the others went to the chapel for morning prayers. When they'd left, she handed me an old dress and a pair of well-worn sandals.

'Wear them in place of your habit.' She didn't look at me.

A nun escorted me to the station where she gave me a railway ticket to Mandalay and left without a word of comfort. Coldly dispatched like a pair of discarded shoes, I sat on a bench and waited for the train.

My thoughts wandered back to the time we were escaping from my father. Then too, I'd waited for the train, rising from despair to joy. Now I fell from joy to utter hopelessness. *Will the train ever come?* The waiting was intolerable. *Why do so many events in my life revolve around a train?*

Fortunately, unlike Louise-Clare, whose parents had left for the UK, I still had my family in Mandalay.

The train steamed into the station, hissing like a venomous snake. I clambered aboard and collapsed into a seat. *I'd slunk away from the convent like a criminal. How will things turn out?* My shoulders drooped. Disorientated and lost, I slumped back in a trance-like state as the train gathered speed and left Toungoo far behind. The engine emitted a long, sharp whistle each time it passed a village, warning folk not to cross the railway line. Paddy fields and teak forests skimmed past.

Dawn crawled to the window and the winter sun rose. The green fields awakened a renewed interest in life, reviving memories of my childhood.

After a few hours, the beauty of life and an almost painful desire to experience its joys overcame me. I stuck my head out of the window, letting the wind play on my face. The train crossed several bridges as it sped towards Mandalay. Desolation rushed upon me once again. *How will I bridge the gap from a religious life to a secular one?*

Sugar cane plantations stretched for kilometres on either side of the track. The train drew up at Pyinmana, where my uncle Pat used to work as a guard. Outside the station, tea shops and stalls lined the main road. Passengers bought food and drinks but I could not bring myself to buy anything without permission from another!

The train stopped at several stations along the way. Vendors stood at the station displaying their trays of food and bottled drinks. Hunger gnawed at my stomach and thirst consumed me, for I'd left without breakfast. Not having used money for so long, I was too timid to buy anything to appease my hunger or quench my thirst. The five hundred kyats lay untouched at the bottom of my bag. I withdrew my head from the window and, shrinking back on the seat, contemplated my future. *What lies ahead for me? How will I earn my living? Will it be possible to get back my old job in the Burma Railways?*

The whiff of eau de cologne from one of the passengers brought back memories of my mother. Confident she'd welcome me with open arms, a surge of relief flooded me. Nothing exceeds the joy of revisiting loved ones and familiar faces. Clasping my hands to my chest, my anticipation mingled with a dread of the future.

With a hiss of steam and a harsh grinding of brakes, the train grumbled to a halt at Mandalay. I alighted with nervous expectation, searching for my mother among the crowd. Mum, Rose and Winston stood on the station platform. A criss-cross of tiny wrinkles fanned out from the corner of my mother's face, revealing her worry. However, her welcoming hug reassured me of her love.

I turned to Rose and Winston and immediately sensed their disappointment. Their looks betrayed their feelings. They'd been proud of me when I joined the convent, but now I'd let them down. People in Burma tended to look upon a person's departure from religious life as a stigma. A pang transfixed me at the thought of my aspirations, all extinguished now—of my sweet, transient hopes burned to ashes. Utter hopelessness overcame me once more.

***

The state had taken over Missionary schools, so it was difficult to obtain employment as a teacher. I visited my old Burma Railway Office but all correspondence was now in Burmese. Tightness in my chest gripped me. I clenched my jaw. There were no social services in Burma and I'd imposed an unnecessary burden on my family by coming home. Feelings of being unwanted and unloved sprang up within me like mushrooms.

Self-conscious of my short hair, one of the first things I did was to visit a hairdresser. After having worn a habit for eight years, my bare legs and uncovered head felt half-naked and exposed to the vulgar gazes of strangers. When attending daily Mass with my mother, all eyes appeared to converge like wheel spokes upon me. Every look of pity or of contempt was like salt on a raw, gaping wound; their glances were slaps upon my face. For so long my life had been ruled by a bell. Now I found myself waiting for its sound to tell me what to do. I needed to be weaned from a captivity that stretched back to those days with my father—his drunkenness, his beatings and cruelty. I'd been a prisoner in my own home.

Like the novice in *The Sound of Music*, I'd longed to walk on the hills in Lashio and Taunggyi. I'd left a good job and entered the novitiate of my own volition, and now all I now owned was the $500 that stood between me and starvation. Both Mum and Rose had teaching positions, so they supported me.

I drifted into a sluggish backwater and could not join the mainstream. My walk, my talk, my downcast eyes, all betrayed me. People seemed to look contemptuously at me as an ex-nun, not knowing I'd left *before* taking the final vows. I yearned for sympathy and understanding, yet shrank from sharing my thoughts with anyone.

Most of my contemporaries had either married or migrated overseas. My dearest friend, Colleen, and her family had left for England as early as 1950. I knew few people. In my loneliness and desperation, whenever I met an eligible bachelor, I wondered if he was the man God intended for me. The priest's farewell words, 'God will reward you for the years you have dedicated to him, and find you a good husband,' rang in my ears. *Where is that man?*

A square peg in a round hole, peace eluded me. I had always known what I wanted but, now unsure of my aims in life, I drifted along like a boat without a rudder. God had told me I was not suited as a nun—that He had other plans in store for me. *Why had He taken so long to tell me this?*

Dazed, bewildered and longing to experience all the good things I'd been deprived of for so many years in the convent, I wanted to make up for my lost time, but seemed incapable of any sense of pleasure. Life in the convent had kept my mental development static. Taught to be dependent on my superiors and develop a child-like simplicity, I now felt like a simpleton and behaved irrationally. My eyes strayed to the floor unless consciously kept from drifting. Even then I looked without seeing, as if my sub-conscious was telling me it was wrong to let my thoughts and eyes wander. Parts of my personality had atrophied, others became immature. It was important to restore the right balance within myself.

I knew little about love and marriage, and wondered what transpired between a man and a woman. No one had ever told me about the secrets of sex and marriage. I longed to listen, look, experiment and learn about life before it passed me by. At nights, sleep encircled me in a suffocating embrace, transmuting thoughts to dreams, mocking me, filling me with dread of the future.

***

When I was still in the novitiate, Mum had written, asking the nuns to find my sister a teaching position at one of their schools. By then, Rose had completed her Diploma in Teacher's Education and Mum wanted her daughter to be in a safe environment, away from a wealthy Buddhist who'd been wooing her.

The nuns gave Rose a job at Namtu in the Shan States. She spent a year teaching there, removed from the source of temptation and mingling with the daughters of wealthy Shans who owned silver mines. At the end of the academic year, unable to tolerate the secluded life at a convent, she returned to Mandalay and found employment at St. Joseph's Convent, her old alma mater.

Mum realised she no longer had the power to restrict her daughter but she wanted her to marry a good Catholic boy. She could only hope and pray. Rose had now grown up, and would have been a delightful companion to me. However, totally ignorant of the ways of the world, I proved unsuitable.

I'd been drilled to walk demurely, with downcast eyes. Ashamed of my awkward manner, Rose tried to show me how to walk correctly. She also taught me modern songs like:

Whatever will be, will be,
The future's not ours to see...

She introduced me to Ann, a well-known Mandalay socialite, who threw lavish parties. She took me pillion riding on her cycle to the public swimming pool, where we cooled off from the heat and dust of Mandalay. Whenever her students gave her free movie passes, Rose took Mum, Winston and me along. My sister loved beautiful clothes and her wardrobe was filled with tailor-made frocks. As we both wore the same size, she gave me some of her dresses.

Then she met Henry, a good-looking German, who held a lucrative position and escorted her to beer-gardens and exclusive clubs. With a snap of his fingers he had waiters running to him. Rose loved luxury and adored what money could buy. I accompanied her to beer-gardens, but found no joy in it. Entrenching myself behind the smoke of a freshly lighted cigarette, I tried to dispel my boredom and frustration, only to choke on its poisonous fumes.

Rose tried to help me adapt to life in the world. However after a while, she no longer went to Ann's parties, and left me to fend for myself. We grew estranged. Each new incident increased our distance in geometrical progression.

Suspecting that Rose did not relish the thought of launching me back into the world, I asked Mum why she no longer went to dances.

'Rose says that you embarrass her and she'd rather go for a drive with Henry.'

Years later, my sister told me that she'd gone to parties at Henry's place and didn't want me tagging along.

Even little Winston had changed. Realising that the family had applied for permission to migrate to the United Kingdom and that his studies in Burma would not be recognised in England, he spent the evenings roaming the streets with his friends, and come home late at nights. My heart ached to see the transformation in my little brother.

I abhorred crowds. Still, realising the need to mingle in society, I continued going to parties. Ann took me under her wing and invited me to all her *soirées*. She also taught me the Cha Cha and the Twist. 'Imagine you're drying your back after stepping out from a bath, and holding a towel in both hands, moving your body in time to the music.'

Ann arranged for a friend to pick me up from home and drop me back afterwards.

I tried to adapt to the new lifestyle, but felt terribly out of place. Awkward and embarrassed, I hoped the earth would open up and swallow me. My days filled with boredom, I wanted independence and needed to be myself, to live my own life. Having done three years of study in the convent, and passed Part A of the Intermediate Exams with distinctions in English, I only needed to complete one year more to get my Bachelor of Arts degree. I decided to continue my university studies.

Even then, the joy of learning eluded me.

Mum remained a pillar of strength and lost no time in searching for some form of employment for me. She had a special devotion to the Blessed Virgin Mary and only wore blue or white, Our Lady's colours.

My mother drew her strength from her devotions, and after three months of trying to find a position for me, she secured me a teaching position at a small school not yet taken over by the State. From then on, my life became a bit more tolerable.

***

Bertie had already taken out work permits for Rose and Winston. He immediately proceeded to get one for me. However, he could only obtain a work permit to train as a student nurse. He wrote, saying that nurses were in great demand in England, and work-permits easy to obtain. Wages in England were good in relation to those in Burma and he would be happy to get me a permit to work in the UK.

Although keen to be re-united with Bertie, I could not see myself emptying bed-pans. The nuns had utilised my teaching talents, and I wanted to be a teacher, not a nurse. Apprehensive of the political situation in Burma, I longed to take wing and fly off, just as Bertie had done. There were no restrictions on the type of work undertaken by migrants to Australia, and I'd be free to teach 'Down Under'. I applied for admission to Australia, intending to go to England only if my application for Australia failed. Despite the long years spent in the convent, I had not lost my initiative.

Mum, Rose and Winston then decided to also apply for admission into Australia, where the people were more easy-going and tolerant of foreign nationals. However, the Department of Immigration rejected their application.

There was no alternative but to rely on Bertie to get both Rose and Winston into England, since Mum refused to go anywhere without her two youngest children. Mum had retained her British passport and could live and work in the UK without a work permit. However, we had to get a Certificate of Identity and apply for clearance from the Police and Tax Offices before leaving the country. Without a Burmese passport, we forfeited the right to live in Burma and could *never* return to live in Burma.

I doubted if we would ever want to return to the land of our birth and looked forward to a new life in Australia.

Chapter 20

The Storm

Teaching opened up a new future. The unyielding time-table and the merciless training of the mind to remove worldly thoughts were all behind me and I was now able to contribute towards my board. A cool breeze played among the leaves of the poinciana tree as Mum and I strolled along the banks of the moat after a day's work.

Mum stopped walking and turned to me. 'I'll be sorry to leave Burma.'

My eyes opened wide. 'Don't you *want* to join Bertie?'

'I do, but my friends, a good job and my own home are here. The Cathedral is only within walking distance. It's so lovely to go to Mass in the mornings and to hear the Angelus pealing out at noon.'

'You can teach in the UK. You have a British passport and the pay is so much better than here. Many of your old friends are there too.'

Mum sighed. 'Life over there'll be hard. English winters are cold and wet.'

'Sit by the heater and remain indoors during winter. Bertie says everyone wears a thick overcoat when outside. Shops, offices and houses are heated.'

'The British out here refer to us as *coffee au lait*. In England, Anglo-Indians are referred to as *blacks*. We'll have to put up with racial prejudice. How would we react under such treatment?'

On our return home from the walk, I asked Winston, 'Are you looking forward to leaving Burma?'

'Don't mind going to England, but hope Mum starts moving soon. All I care for is to have a good time. The UK has more work and better wages.'

Years later, Rose told me that she had longed for a new life in a new country with a good Catholic boy. Her dream-boy was tall, fair-haired and fair-skinned with blue eyes, and she hoped to find one in England.

As a British national, Mum could leave Burma whenever she wished. However, wanting the best for us, she had sacrificed her needs to help improve our prospects abroad. The Burmese government delayed issuing Clearance Papers from the Department of Taxation. The Department of Police and the Immigration Department, too, postponed issuing our Certificates of Identity so Bertie had to renew the work permits for Rose and Winston every six months, time after time.

The forms seemed endless. Always one more to be filled, always one more fee to be paid. Each application form brought its own frustration and tension within our family.

We had just had afternoon tea and were clearing the table when a stranger knocked at our door, saying he wished to see Rose. As she was out with Henry, Mum told me to entertain the visitor while he waited for her. After so many years of silence and refraining from trivial talk in a convent, it was hard for me to socialise.

Yet Mum wanted me to overcome my innate shyness. 'What better way is there for you to learn how to socialise than to converse with a man of the world?'

At her insistence, I left my bedroom and went to meet him. Mandalay folk knew everything about each other and indulged in idle gossip with a voracious appetite, so he was aware of my having been a novice at a convent. Ralph was several years older than me, and had been educated at a private school. He was an employee of the American Consulate, and his knowledge of world politics was extensive. He spoke about the political situation in Burma.

'I've been out of touch with current affairs, and know absolutely nothing of such topics,' I said.

'Don't let that worry you. I'll lend you some copies of *Newsweek*. You'll soon catch up on things.' He visited us again the following weekend and brought me a few copies of *Newsweek*. I devoured the magazines and learned of Mao Tse-tung's Cultural Revolution, his Red Guards, the strained relations between India and Pakistan and the alignment of Peking with Pakistan. 'Burma is not only torn by Civil War, but is sandwiched between two countries on the brink of war,' I said on returning the magazines during his next visit.

Ralph handed me fresh copies. 'Yes, but read these. They're the latest issues and will bring you up-to-date with the news.'

I managed to speak on a one-to-one basis with Ralph, but still needed to learn how to associate with others and engage in small talk. While the rest of the globe continued in turmoil, I tried to come to terms with a world which had been hidden from me. Mum advised me to mingle, to have fun and friends and catch up on the things missed during my novitiate days. I continued going to Ann's parties and frequently met Ralph there.

'I need to relax after a heavy week of work,' he explained. 'My wife is at home with the kids.'

One day he asked, 'Would you like to tutor the American Consul's two children? Mrs Metson, the Consul's wife has asked me to find a tutor for her daughters. They've been doing a correspondence course from the United States, but need a teacher to go through the notes with them.'

'I'd love that.'

Through Ralph's recommendation, Mrs Metson gave me the job. A chauffeur picked me up from home and dropped me off at the American consulate. The luxury of a posh car, where the chauffeur graciously opened the door for me, projected a feeling of opulence.

A visit by the famous astronaut, John Glenn, the first American to be launched into space and orbit the earth three times, created a stir in Mandalay. The reception for him was a privilege granted to only a few. However, thanks to Ralph, Rose and I received an invitation to the reception held at the American Consulate in his honour.

I was thrilled to shake hands with John Glenn, who presented me with a personally signed replica of his space craft. A souvenir I treasured highly.

Weeks passed. Ralph's hobby was photography. He asked Mum whether he could take a few photos. Mum consented, and our friendship blossomed with Mum's blessing. Then the inevitable occurred.

Ralph had brought over some more magazines. 'I love you,' he announced. 'Will you accept me and my two daughters if I get a divorce? My wife and I are not compatible. She doesn't understand me.'

I had never intended to fall for him or to cause a break-up of his marriage, but I imagined that fate had thrown us together for some obscure reason. Ralph being the only man I knew at the time, the prospect sounded feasible. I was aware of the Pauline Privilege permitting a married man to marry in the Catholic faith provided he received Baptism and became a Catholic.

'Have you ever been baptised?' I asked. *If he has already baptised, then marriage with him is out of the question.*

'I was educated at a Christian school but was never baptised. I'm willing to do anything that is required.'

As soon as he left, I confided our plans to Mum. She held onto the table to steady herself. 'How can you break up a marriage?'

'But his marriage was already on the rocks. Anyway, it was you who encouraged our friendship in the first place.'

Mum turned pale, but said nothing further. She lost no time in seeing Father Manier, the parish priest. He immediately sent for me.

I left home, armed and ready for the combat I anticipated.

His eyes opened wide as they probed into the depths of my soul. 'Is all this true?'

'Yes, Father. I hoped you'd write to the Pope and ask for the Pauline Privilege.'

The priest shook his head. He looked like John the Baptist with his black beard and gaunt appearance. Yet despite his forbidding figure he did not talk of fire and brimstone. He stroked his beard. 'I refuse to write to the Pope for you. Break off your friendship immediately.'

Having practised obedience in the convent for so many years, I did not question his words. On Ralph's first visit after that interview with the priest, I said, 'This to be our final meeting. I will not see you again. The priest has refused permission for the marriage.'

After a long silence, he said, 'May I kiss you farewell?'

We kissed and embraced for the first time but delayed the departure and lingered on, reluctant to part.

The next morning, Winston said, 'We watched you and Ralph last night.'

'Where were you?'

He grinned. 'We climbed my bedroom wall and had a good view of you.'

My embarrassment knew no bounds but his frank admission pleased me.

Fortunately, a short time later, the Australian embassy sent me a letter accepting my application as a migrant. Having only a few months left for my final exams, I delayed my departure. While I lingered in limbo to complete my university degree, Rose, too, waited for her Certificate of Identity.

One day, Mum called me aside. 'Henry has invited Rose and you to Maymyo for the weekend.'

My eyebrows shot up in surprise. 'But Rose has been going out alone with him for some time now. She can go on her own. I *don't* want to go.'

'Please go,' Mum insisted. 'I need you to act as chaperone. It wouldn't look good for a young girl to spend a night out with a man. People will talk.'

My sister would be the talk of the town if I didn't accompany her. Besides, it was always difficult to refuse my Mother anything. Hoping to break the monotony of my life, I consented.

Henry drove us up to Maymyo in his Volkswagen. To make a foursome, Rose introduced me to a Catholic boy. He was an old flame of my sister's—young and good-looking. I wasn't attracted to him but hoped he'd help me forget Ralph and the muddle I'd got into. He wanted more than just kissing and hugging, however, so I broke off the friendship.

My sister must have taken offence at that, because the chasm between us grew deeper. Time passed. I thanked God for sorting out my life and opening a door for me into Australia.

I'll never forget the time our doorbell rang, and Winston answered the door. He hurried to me. 'It's Ralph's son.'

My mouth flew open. Ralph had a teenage son, besides two little girls. Not wanting to have anything more to do with him, I had no wish to meet his son. I sprang to my feet, raced to the door and slammed it in his face.

That was a mistake. The boy threw stones at our door. The solid timber door could not suffer damage from them, but the neighbours would soon turn out to watch.

Unable to bear the thought of a scandal, Rose said, 'You should let the boy in and hear what he has to say.'

Winston nodded his assent. I looked at Mum for advice but, face contorted in agony, she avoided my gaze. We let him in.

The young man glared at me. 'My father's been drinking.'

'Who are you?' I pretended not to know him.

'I'm Sid. Ralph's son. He's been drinking and was still drinking when I left.'

I cut him short. 'That's not *my* concern. *You* stop him. You're old enough.'

'Come and see what damage you've done to our family.'

'No.' My voice rose in anger.

Winston was now on his feet. I had no wish to see my brother get into a fight, especially as Sid was so much older.

The boy stood, hand on hip, leaning forward and making his point with a belligerent forefinger. 'I'm *not* leaving without you.'

Looking around for support, the only eye contact I had was Winston's. He appeared to be spoiling for a fight.

Sid's eyes were ablaze. I had a flashing mental image of my father when he was angry. *What should I do?* I didn't want to see Ralph, and neither did I wish Winston to throw the visitor out physically in case it developed into a fight.

Rose slid up to me and whispered, 'The neighbours will hear everything.'
I hesitated, unable to make up my mind.

Winston broke the stalemate. 'I think you'd better go, Sid.' He sounded surprisingly calm.

'No. I won't go without your sister. She must come. I won't leave until she comes.'

'I'll come with you if you like,' Winston offered.

'No. I only want your sister,' Sid shouted.

I turned on him in a fury. 'I'll only come if Winston accompanies me. Either that, or get out of our house.'

'All right.' He strode to the door, but checked to see whether I'd followed.

I stepped outside with Winston. He had taken up weight-lifting and was strong for his age. I felt safe with him.

We walked in silence. With Sid on one side and Winston on the other, I imagined myself a prisoner being dragged to the docks. *I'll go and put a stop to everything there and then.*

***

On our arrival at Ralph's house, Sid asked us to come straight in. His mother had been expecting me.

'This is my mother. That's Hazel and her brother.'

'Come,' she said, 'Come and look at what you've done.' Taking us into an inner room, she pointed to her husband. 'Look at *that*.'

The room was in semi-darkness, but in the corner, was an easy-chair where Ralph slouched, drunk and dishevelled. Even from that distance I smelt the alcohol. His face sagged as if unable to hold itself erect with the weight of the drink. A vacant stare at an invisible spot on the wall indicated he was completely stoned.

The sight of him in that state brought back visions of my father. I stared at him, overcome with revulsion and devoid of any stirring of pity. *He had descended so low.*

I turned to leave the room, and came face-to-face with his wife.

'See what you've done to him. To our family.'

I tried to formulate an answer, but it wouldn't come.

'You're welcome to have him. Just take him and leave me and my children in peace. I don't care for him anymore.'

I started to say something, but she cut me short.

'I'll never interfere with you. I promise. Just get him out of my sight.'

***

We walked home, shrouded in silence. The world outside did not exist. Her words kept ringing in my ears. Thoughts raced from one side of my brain to the other. My feet dragging, my head heavy with a strange sense of foreboding, I went to bed as soon as we returned home. Darkness only brought an abyss of anguish.

The following day when sober, Ralph came to apologise. He looked drawn and depressed. 'What a wreck my marriage is. I swear I'll never drink if you marry me.'

Torn with pity for him, I felt myself weaken. *What use is a drunken husband to the woman anyway? Perhaps he will reform if I marry him?* How gullible I was!

Instead of stopping my ears to his pleas, I said, 'I'll be leaving for Australia, but you may join me if you want.' He had a very good position at the American Consul, and I realised he'd never get such an excellent job. *Perhaps that would deter him.*

'I'll follow you to the ends of the earth if you put me in touch with some correspondence courses in accounting, when you get to Australia. I'd like to study accounting and get a position as an accountant. We'll live comfortably with my two little girls. My wife could return to her parents. My son is now old enough to support himself.'

It seemed feasible to me at the time, even though I preferred the two girls to remain with their mother. *Perhaps the priests in Australia will be more lenient, and write to the Pope for permission to marry in Church.*

The next day, I received a letter from Mum. 'If you wish to continue living with me, you are not to meet Ralph at my house.'

Mum had never laid down the law so firmly. *She should realise I intend saving his soul and the soul of his two children. I have no intention of quitting home and being his mistress. Any permanent relationship has to first begin by a church marriage and God's blessing. I will never meet Ralph again.* These thoughts ran through the corridors of my mind, but I did not voice them.

On his next visit, I told him he was not welcome at our house.

***

Ralph continued to attend Ann's parties, where we talked and danced as friends. He always treated me with the utmost respect. He liked slow dances, but, unable to cope with fast dance music, the Beatles' hits forced him to the sidelines.

My desire to leave the country deepened. *Why had I ever left the Convent where the community had spun a cocoon of kindness around me? The simple life had brought me inner happiness, and I had taken each day as a gift of God.* All I could do now was to pray and wait. I deluded myself into thinking that God wanted me to marry Ralph and convert him and his two daughters. Once again, I lost my peace of mind.

Throughout my early life, I'd learned to survive danger. Despite that, the cold hand of fear gripped my heart.

Chapter 21

Partings

The year dragged on. I was now teaching at a small private school which the Burmese government had overlooked when requisitioning larger and wealthier Christian schools. By the end of the year, it was taken over and I was transferred to St. Joseph's Convent—the same high school I had attended soon after the war. It held fond memories for me. The school had been renamed No. 8 State High School. Fortunately, English was still taught there, even though Burmese was replacing it, commencing from the lower grades. I realised the language requirement would mean I'd soon be unable to teach.

As our Certificates of Identity were still delayed, Rose and Henry flew to Rangoon, hoping to speed up the process. Henry's contract with the government was coming to an end, and they hoped to leave Burma together.

The snail-like sluggishness of officialdom frustrated us. But just as our patience reached breaking point, the Certificates of Identity arrived.

Rose sold as many things as possible. I bought her bicycle—my only means of transport. With Henry's help Rose was able to take all her valuables. As an employee of a West German firm, he obtained diplomatic immunity so his luggage did not have to go through customs. Her jewellery thus slipped through unchallenged.

Each individual was permitted only seventy-five English pounds and a thin gold chain. When Mum and I left Burma later, we had to give away whatever remained unsold.

Mum tried to smuggle out two thousand kyats to Bertie through

Eugene, the son of an old school friend, Nellie Rogers. The money was then worth four hundred Australian dollars. It never reached my brother. Eugene betrayed my mother's trust, and probably used it to pay his own fare to Perth in Western Australia.

***

Rose and Henry flew out of Rangoon on 6 December, 1966. Some years later when we met again, she said, 'As our plane circled overhead, the spire of the Shwedagon Pagoda pointed at the sky like a warning finger, daring us never to return. I spent a few days in Rome with Henry. He saw me off at the airport when I left for London, then he flew to his home in Germany. Bertie welcomed me at the airport and took me to stay with some of his friends for the night. I looked out from the window of my room at a sea of faces on the street. Everyone had fair complexions and light hair. The next day, I reported for work at the Queen Mary's Hospital for Children and was shown to the nurses' quarters. The student nurses were cold and unfriendly. In Burma, I had a flock of admirers but this hospital only employed female staff. After a couple of months, I applied for a transfer to Horton Hospital.'

Breathless with excitement, Rose continued her story. 'Within a month, I met Pat, an Irish Catholic. Broad shouldered, blond and blue-eyed, he was quiet and reserved. I pictured him as an ideal husband, the perfect man to father my children. During our holidays, we went to Ireland to meet his parents in County Cork. We visited Blarney Castle and kissed the famous stone.'

Both Rose and Pat were loquacious enough before, but now no one could stop their incessant chatter. A strong bond grew between the two, during their holiday in the lovely countryside around County Cork.

***

We were unable to obtain British passports as our father had taken Burmese citizenship. Non-British citizens wishing to work in Britain needed work permits, and Winston's was nearing expiry. He had nothing to hold him back and was glad to leave, knowing he'd be with Bertie, who took the place of the father he barely remembered.

Winston had been only four when we had left Rangoon in 1952, so Mum asked me to accompany him to the city. She was afraid to see him off at Rangoon so said goodbye to him in Mandalay, where she had friends to protect her from her ex-husband.

The flight to Rangoon early in 1967 was Winston's first plane trip. Having spent most of his life in sleepy Mandalay, he stared wonder-eyed at the bright lights of the capital. His gaze smouldered with intensity. 'There's nothing like this in Mandalay!'

My heart warmed towards him, remembering the days I'd cared for him as an infant. 'How are you feeling?'

'I'm looking forward to fun and adventure. I want to live—not simply to exist. I wonder what London will be like.' His eyes gleamed and I realised that, even now, he was finding it difficult to adjust to what lay before him.

The time approached to bid farewell. *Will we ever meet each other again?* In my mind's eye, I saw Winston as a toddler of two. His temperature had soared.

The doctor shook his head, and said, 'The child has food poisoning.'

Little Winston survived, but his legs turned as thin as broomsticks, and he was left so weak that he couldn't rise from his bed.

I also recalled the time when a hit-and-run car had knocked him off his bicycle, leaving him where he'd fallen, pale and unconscious.

He must have had nine lives, because later on in Australia he would come to have a near-death experience.

A lump rose to my throat as he entered the plane. I watched it lift off from the tarmac. *How will he fare in England?*

Years later, Winston told me that, as the plane sped down the run-way, he had peered through the window, searching for my lone figure. 'All I saw was the golden pagoda sparkling in the morning sun. I arrived in England a few months after Rose. Once there, I reported for work at Longrove Hospital and enrolled as a student-nurse. It took some time to adjust but I eventually found friends.'

***

As a British subject, Mum could not sell her house because all foreigners had to forfeit their property to the State, if they left Burma. But Mum needed the money from the sale of her house to pay for our airfares to London, so she took Burmese citizenship and sold the property to the first person who made her an offer. Then Mum resumed her British passport. The interim period between the sale of the house and the arrival of Mum's British passport served to renew the strong bond between us.

I hoped to fly out to Perth after my university exams, and was willing to take any job while waiting for a teaching position in West Australia. The Socialist Government frowned upon anyone associating with capitalists, so the necessity to leave grew more urgent. Through the grapevine, I came to know that I was black-listed by the Burmese military for having attended the reception in honour of John Glenn at the American Consulate and for teaching the Consul's children.

I longed to be free of the web which had enmeshed me, but felt myself being sucked into a vortex of uncontrollable events. A deep-seated fear nagged me. *Will I be held back against my will?*

On returning home after leaving Winston at the Rangoon airport, I found the house empty and cold, with only Mum and my memories for company. Echoes of my siblings' happy voices in post-war Mandalay filled the air. My imagination roamed unbridled. I pictured Rupert returning from the grave with the grinning Japanese skull, Bertie strumming his guitar and singing his favourite songs, Rose filling the air with her songs. Strains of *April Love, Catch a Falling Star, The Lion Sleeps Tonight*, and *Love Letters in the Sand* drifted across my mind.

The stillness in the house reminded me of my novitiate days. Now, everything at home remained in ghostly silence too. No books lined the shelves. We'd given them away to friends. Gone were the mementoes of some of the most turbulent times in Burma's history. All the items, so treasured, had vanished. The place stood stark and bare. We'd sold whatever possible.

I gazed at the empty rooms and the naked shelves. Even our radio had gone. Rubbish bins overflowed with litter; heavy luggage strapped and locked. Smaller items remained to be packed later. Only my clothes and a few souvenirs were to accompany me into my new world.

By now, Mum and I had resigned from our teaching positions. We made the most of our time together and attended church daily, hoping and praying everything would go according to plan. All we could do was to trust in God and hope for the best.

In the evenings, we went for walks along the road surrounding Fort Dufferin. As we strolled, hand-in-hand, the walls of the fort frowned down upon us. Grass glistened and birds chorused to the blushing sky. Water hyacinth spread its rafts of mauve, hiding the deep water below. When tired, we rested beneath the shade of the tamarind trees, drinking sugar-cane juice during the long, hot summer.

A cloak of languor enveloped the city, bestowing a false sense of security. I ached to see as much of Burma as possible before leaving the country, but travel was precarious during the sixties because of the Civil War. Despite the danger, I went on a short tour of the Inle Lake with its famous leg rowers.

Mum's passport came through in July, nearly six months after Winston's departure. My legs felt rubbery and my stomach did backflips. I accompanied her to Rangoon. Our hearts were oppressed by anguish at our parting, but we knew we were doing the right thing. Burma was a country rent by a civil war even now tearing us apart. It was no longer a land of peaceful pagodas. The place was in a state of turmoil with late night curfews. Armed soldiers roamed the streets. Universities—hotbeds of political agitation—remained closed.

On Mum's last day, we took a pony cart to the Scott Market and bought ivory and teak carvings of elephants. We were unlikely to meet again. Few words passed between us now. All the things I ached to say remained dammed up in a water-tight wall within me. I made vain attempts at being cheerful. We had been together even under Japanese occupation, but now the Burmese government had succeeded in splitting our family. Mum no longer sang. We feared my father would try to ruin her plans and were afraid he'd turn up at the airport, like the proverbial bad penny, to harm her or thwart her plans to leave Burma.

On a cloudy day in July, the day of Mum's departure finally arrived. Numb with grief at our imminent separation, we scarcely spoke. The time for parting was very close and speech was needless. Seeing Mum's face tight with anxiety, my heart twisted in knots. *Mum will be arriving in London during the middle of winter. How will she feel?*

Poised between a turbulent past and a promising future, time seemed to disappear in the dusky sunlight. One by one, like fledgling birds, we had spread our wings, taking flight from the land of our birth. I remained watching as the plane, a dwindling and forlorn speck in the sky, slid behind the darkening sky. Long shadows signalled the end of the day. Soon the grumble of thunder reminded me of returning home. *Where was home?* I was in the middle of nowhere—a stranger in an unsettled country. My eyes filled with unshed tears and my heart convulsed with grief at Mum's departure. I traced my steps back to the taxi stand, and took a taxi back to the city to stay with my aunt and uncle. There I waited, with bated breath, for news of Mum's safe arrival in the UK, wondering whether my turn would ever come before the doors closed forever.

Russia had its iron curtain and China its bamboo curtain. *What barrier will Burma surround itself with? Perhaps barbed wire?*

I shuddered.

Chapter 22

All Alone

After Mum's departure, I remained all alone in what appeared to be a God-forsaken country. My family had departed, but I consoled myself by thinking that the same sun rose over us wherever we were.

My uncle worked as a mathematics professor and was also the Dean of one of the colleges. He and his family lived in a cottage on the university campus. My cousins had been my childhood companions, but we had dissimilar interests now—our respective religions keeping us apart. As children, we'd accepted each other as cousins, never thinking of our different religions or cultural backgrounds. Now the boys avoided speaking to me. The girls, too, seemed uneasy in my presence. Only my aunt and uncle talked to me.

Tina, the eldest cousin, who'd been closer in age to June, spoke to me once. 'Do you have a photo of June?'

'No. We lost our photos during the war. Did you manage to save your family photo album?'

'We evacuated before Rangoon was bombed and managed to take most of our things with us to Mandalay. I have a photo of June. Would you like to see it?'

My heart leapt. *How I'd love to see my sister's photo!*

I could scarcely resist my tears when Tina showed me a photo taken during our last holiday before the war. There was June, Rupert and Bertie along with my father, aunt and cousins. Mum had insisted that the climb up the hill was too difficult for her, and I was too little to do it.

'Would you like to keep them?' Tina said.

Tears filled my eyes as I threw my arms around her, grateful for my beloved sister's photo.

In a desert of loneliness, I waited for the necessary papers to leave the country. Apart from mealtimes, I spent most of my days wandering around in the university gardens, recalling the times we visited our cousins on Sundays. The final examinations for my Bachelor of Arts degree were only three months away.

I was fated never to complete my studies in Rangoon. Students rioted; the army called in and the university was closed. A clash ensued and some students died. My uncle, the mathematics professor, had to flee for his life from his burning car.

I stood poised on a razor's edge, teetering between utter ruin and life in a new world. The serpent of doubt raised its ugly head. I'd watched my family leave Burma one by one. Within me lingered a germ of foreboding that I'd be trapped by some terrible stroke of fate. Unbidden thoughts strained at the chords of my heart. A sense of being spied upon hung over me like a dark cloud. I nervously awaited news of my Certificate of Identity, suffering tortures of suspense, imagining the worst.

In August, a letter arrived, informing me that my papers awaited collection at Rangoon airport. I looked heavenwards and made the sign of the cross. Then I wrote to Ralph, informing him of the date of my departure. Fearing that my father would attempt to molest me or thwart my plans to leave at the last minute, Mum had paid for Ralph's flight from Mandalay, so he could see me off.

Three days before leaving, there was a knock at the door. As no one else was around, I opened it. My father stood before me. His brow was lined; his hair grey. He looked older than his 67 years. His deep set eyes were circled by dark rings. I recognised his hooked nose.

I had dreaded this, hoping to slip out of the country without ever meeting him again, but Aunt Jhan must have informed him of my impending departure. All my fears came rushing back. Mingled with my fear, contempt welled up from the depths of my being, bringing to mind the merciless beatings and unwarranted condemnation he'd heaped upon my mother. Taking a deep breath, I drew myself upright and backed away, hoping he daren't harm me in his sister's home.

'Hello Hazel.' He stepped into the house as if invited; obviously seeing my action as a welcome, not a rejection.

'Hello.'

He smirked. 'How are things with you?'

'Fine.'

'Been a long time since I've seen any of the family,' he said, trying to initiate a conversation.

I remained silent, with only an occasional mumble.

'You know, whatever I did was for the best for all of you.'

'But you drank. You beat Mum and were unfaithful to her.'

'Oh come on. A little strapping never hurt anyone.'

'How would *you* know? You were drunk every evening.' My voice rose.

'What's the harm in a drink or two?'

I knew he had come to reinstate himself in my eyes and to justify his actions. Fear slipped off from my shoulders like a cloak. 'You peeked at me while I was having a shower!'

He coloured, shuffling his feet on the bare floor.

'You peeped through the hole in the bathroom wall while I was undressed,' I continued, driving my point home.

'I was only trying to find out if you were ready for marriage.'

His actions and words had thundered out in the past and I bore the mental scars of his abuse. Now he sounded like a desperate man, but he failed to arouse my slightest sympathy.

My lip curled and a bitter taste rose to my mouth. 'That was horrible, too horrible for words.'

'I saw nothing,' he continued, after a short pause, obviously waiting for some remark from me; a word of forgiveness or a reproof.

My silence must have irked him. He stopped arguing his case or trying to redeem his name. A forceful person, interaction with others mattered very much to him provided he held all the cards.

He changed tactics. 'Always an oyster, you shut yourself off from me... your father, who fed and clothed you.'

'What a life. Sheer hell!'

'You never showed me any love.'

'What do *you* know of love? All you can understand is possessiveness; to possess one's mind and body with the groping and molesting.'

My father blew his nose with a noise like a cloudburst. Perhaps he was trying to elicit some type of pity from me.

'I struggled to keep your hands off me and lived in fear and dread of you. It was always a silent battle between us. I'm not like Bertie, and can *never* forgive you or forget the past.'

He straightened and dropped the aggrieved-parent mask he wore. 'I'd love to test whether you and your sister are still virgins.'

I turned away from him in disgust, my anger now at fever pitch. I fisted my hand and pushed it hard against my mouth to prevent my lips from quivering. *He hasn't changed. He is still vile and reprehensible!*

He must have realised my heart had hardened against him, because he gave up and wished me goodbye. With a sense of relief, I shook hands, refusing to let him kiss me; glad to see the last of him. I had confronted him and my fear of him was no more.

Little did I realise he would continue to haunt my nightmares for years!

My aunt phoned for a taxi and I left for the airport, gazing out of the vehicle at the old colonial buildings, now shabby and badly in need of a coat of paint. I glanced down at the betel-juice stained pavements and the stinking drains.

Travellers were only permitted to buy their tickets at the airport when they produced their passport or Certificate of Identity. When I reached for my handbag it was missing. I'd been so overcome with excitement at the thought of leaving the country, that I'd mislaid the bag containing my ticket. *Have I lost my sole chance of freedom?* My breathing came fast and furious. *What can I do?* As usual, I prayed and retraced my steps. People dashed past. I took no notice of them.

Five minutes later, panting and gasping for breath, I stumbled to the Burma Airlines counter. 'Excuse me, but have you seen a black handbag?'

The receptionist held up the handbag. 'Is this yours?'

The words sounded like sweet music. Overwhelmed by emotion, I wanted to hug her. But I only thanked her and hurried towards the Customs' counter.

Ralph was waiting to see me off. I greeted him abstractedly and sank back into a chair, recalling stories about delays and disappointments at the airport. *Will I be jailed for associating with American capitalists?* I buried my face in my hands. Although I'd waited stoically during the past weeks, I could stand the strain no longer, and bit my fingernails in desperation.

When my name was called out by Customs, I sprang to my feet, wished Ralph a final farewell and poured out all my Burmese currency into his hands because I was only permitted to take seventy-five pounds out of the country. Strange as it may seem, I had no regrets about leaving him behind. All I thought of was one word—*freedom!*

A custom's official ushered me into a small room. The fans whirred noisily overhead while she searched me for banned items such as drugs, cash or jewellery. I flushed with embarrassment at the groping hands. Taking my gold chain, she weighed it carefully to check if it was heavier than the permitted amount. *God please let it be the correct weight,* I prayed.

Once in the departure lounge, I crossed and re-crossed my legs, counting the number of bricks in the wall and licking my dry lips. The minutes crept by on the old clock by the door.

Finally, the call for boarding came over the loudspeaker. I rose and followed the others, entered the plane and sank into my seat.

Life teemed with possibilities and I longed to explore them. *The spectre of fear would no longer haunt me.*

***

The plane had a stopover at Singapore. Enraptured by the neon signs and city sights, I checked in at the Hotel Singapura, had a refreshing swim in the hotel pool and took a short walk, visiting the shops and taking care not to get lost. Never having been alone in a strange city, a mixture of elation and fright took possession of me. With only seventy five pounds in my possession, I refrained from buying anything in Singapore, hoarding my money, not knowing when I'd be able to start earning my living in Australia.

After dinner at the hotel which was fortunately included in the price of my airline ticket, I had an early night and slept peacefully.

The following morning, I rose early for the final leg of my flight to Perth.

Chapter 23

Perth

The lights of Perth winked a welcome as the plane touched down. I alighted from the aircraft and the wind whipped my skirt as I followed the other passengers to the terminal.

The official from the Immigration Department glanced at my photo and read all the details carefully. He threw me a quick look. 'So you've come to stay, have you?'

My pulse raced. The Burmese Government had not issued me with a passport. *Will my Certificate of Identity be in order?* My voice quivered. 'Yes.'

The officer's smile lit up his whole face, dispelling all my dark fears. 'Welcome to Australia.' He stamped the papers.

Another obstacle remained to be overcome. At Rangoon, a Customs Official had searched me in case the money I carried was more than I professed to have. Another had weighed my gold chain lest it was above the permitted weight. After the ordeal at Rangoon airport, dreading the thought of facing Customs officers, I collected my luggage—a fibre suitcase, and a box made of bamboo matting, containing my entire wardrobe.

I sighed with relief and stepped forward, but was stopped by the Quarantine Official on duty. He glanced at the bamboo box. 'This will have to be fumigated.' His polite face betrayed no trace of disgust at the sight of the shabby-looking thing at my feet. All passengers had already been decontaminated by a masked man who had sprayed everyone and everything in the aircraft cabin before we stepped off the plane onto

Australian soil. It seemed my belongings from the baggage hold would have to be done as well.

Customs finally allowed me to pass. On entering the arrival section of the airport, I started at the sight of men standing around, holding placards. *Was it a political protest? Names were displayed in large letters.*

I sighed with relief. *They were waiting to greet their guests.*

Father Foley had written to say he'd be there at 2 am. Will he be waiting for me? He could have had an accident and not been able to come.

Within seconds, someone with a black soutane and a warm, welcoming smile stepped forward to shake my hand. After a warm greeting, he led me to the car and we drove to my sponsors, Mr and Mrs Samuel. They had agreed to coach me in those little things that made Australia so different from Burma.

The Samuels, an Anglo-Indian family who had come to Australia with the first wave of migrants when Burma attained independence from Britain in 1948, were waiting for me.

After a few hours' sleep, I awoke to breathe in the air of perfect freedom. Sunshine filled the room; the terrors of the past faded into insignificance. Life was full of promise. I arose from bed in a mood matching the sunbeams laughing on the walls. The sky was a mass of gold and crimson as the sun burst over the horizon. Oh, the unspeakable bliss of the sunlit day with its promise of a new life!

Vera, the eldest girl, gave me a woollen overcoat, as I'd arrived in August with only a cardigan to keep myself warm. She also showed me where to catch the city bus and register for employment. My steps quickened as I set out. While waiting for the bus I glanced around, drinking in the scenery. Unlike the searing heat of Mandalay, the sun shone with welcoming warmth, the trees proudly unfurling the new season's foliage. Some, already dressed in blushing blossoms, awaited the dawn of spring, now only two weeks away. The lullaby of bees among the branches was music to my ears.

I queued up with the others and boarded the bus. Fumbling for the correct change, my purse flew open, scattering its contents on the floor. Embarrassment quickly turned to surprise. Several passengers were down on their hands and knees, searching for the cash. I recoiled with fear, standing helplessly, looking at them gathering up my precious coins. *A familiar fear lurched in me. Are they going to keep my money?* I held my breath…

They handed back every penny with a cheery smile, and my heart immediately went out to the people of Perth.

Once in the city, I joined the columns of pedestrians following the path leading to the Commonwealth Employment Office. Elated, I took my time, looking about in wonder and marvelling at the Australian accents and phrases. Hearing a voice call out, 'Pipers, Pipers,' I scanned the premises in search of the musicians.

A boy stood beside a stack of newspapers, holding a paper out to passers-by.

After registering my name at the Commonwealth Employment Service, my heart sank. *How will I survive once the money runs out? Should I have joined my family in England?* Bertie had assured me of a job there, but my intentions were to continue my university studies, while working as a teacher. *Now I was reduced to seeking employment in any job.* As a new migrant in Perth with only seventy-five pounds sterling in my pocket, the absolute necessity of finding employment as soon as possible, weighed down upon me. The days turned to weeks. I wore out the pavements of Perth going for work interviews. I applied for a position as a teacher in a Catholic Girls' College at Perth, only to be informed it was the end of the school year and most vacancies for the following term had already been filled.

A fortnight later, not wishing to impose upon the Samuels for long, but still without work and desperate for a job, I moved into a hostel not far from the city. Fortunately, the Employment Bureau sent me a cheque to tide me over.

Shortly after, seeing an advertisement for a receptionist, I applied for the position, and obtained an interview at a small office of a warehouse in an industrial area. Butterflies flitted in my stomach.

The interviewer, a short squat man with a foreign accent, asked, 'What experience have you had, my dear?'

'I've just arrived in Australia,' I replied, evading the question.
'How long have you been in Perth?'
My knees trembled. 'Just a few weeks.'
'Do you have any friends or relatives here?' His blue eyes seemed to bore straight through me.
My cheeks grew hot. 'None.' By now I was certain I would not get the job.
'There's not much work to do—send invoices and answer the phone,' he said. 'The wages are basic, but I think you'll suit me.'
My heart leaped. 'When would you like me to start, Sir?'
His name was Podoski. 'Just call me Ski, my dear.' He stretched out his hand. 'What about 9 am tomorrow?'
I beamed. 'That'll be fine.'
The next day, Ski gave me a pile of invoices to send out. 'I have to meet clients and will be away most of the time.'
Isolated in a large building with no female company, I asked, 'Will I be alone in this big building the whole day?'
'No. There's a lady downstairs who works in the warehouse. She receives all deliveries and knows where to store them. She comes in early and remains until 3 pm. I'll be in every afternoon to close the building, so you have nothing to worry about, my dear.'
He smiled and took me downstairs into the warehouse to meet Eliza, the store woman. The room was filled with cartons and smelt of sawdust. Eliza, a big, buxom Russian, looked like she could handle any job. She nodded at me when introduced, saying, 'Come again, anytime you need anything.'
I soon caught up with the work. I joined the Perth City Council library and brought in a book to read after completing all the paperwork. Now, I earned sufficient money to cover my board and lodging, and had so much free time too. It suited me until a more lucrative position turned up.
I slipped downstairs to say hello to Eliza.
'Do you like it here?' she asked.
'There's little work, but I bring a book along.'
'What are you doing here?' She blurted out. 'You're a *good* girl.'

My brows shot up. 'What do you mean?

Eliza placed her hands upon her hips. 'No girl stays long. The boss doesn't need a receptionist. He likes to fool around. He has a wife, but wants to play with young girls.'

'Ski has only taught me the work. He's out most of the time.' My voice trembled.

She shook her head like a shaggy dog. 'Don't stay. Go soon.'

I needed the job. It had taken me weeks to get this position.

The next day, after 3 pm, not long after Eliza had left, Ski came in. 'There's something I need to show you in the warehouse.'

Once downstairs, he ushered me into Eliza's office and shut the door. Assuming he had done that to keep out the dust, I thought nothing of it.

He turned, drew me into his arms and stroked my hair. 'How beautiful you are.' He began pawing me.

Horrified, I pushed him off. 'No. This is not part of my job.'

He seemed surprised, not expecting to be rebuffed by a mere migrant, but he let go of me.

***

I'd been boarding in the Girls' Friendly Society on Adelaide Terrace at the time, and having no one to turn to, mentioned the incident to the Matron at the hostel.

'You should report this to the police,' she advised me.

'I need the money. I'll remain on until the end of the week and get my week's wages.'

She put her hand on my shoulder. 'Take care.'

The next morning, I went downstairs to Eliza and told her how right she'd been. 'I'm leaving after receiving my wages on Friday. Thank you for warning me.'

Eliza smiled. 'I *knew* you were a good girl.'

I had a visitor a bit later on that morning, and guessed the lady was Russian when she introduced herself as the boss's wife. 'How do you like your work?' she asked.

'It's all right, but I'll be leaving tomorrow.'
'But why?'
'I don't feel safe here.'
'Oh, yes. He's always molesting young girls.' She burst into sobs. 'Did he... touch you too?'

I nodded, strengthened in my resolve to leave.

Ski tried the same tactics that afternoon. 'I need you to send some parcels tomorrow. They are downstairs.' He turned to leave.

'Your wife came in this morning.' I felt braver now after speaking to the matron.

He spun around, eyebrows raised. 'What did she want?'

'She asked me whether I'm happy here.' I watched his reaction.

The man turned grey. 'What did you say?'

'That I didn't feel safe.'

'Why?'

'Because of what happened yesterday.'

He slapped his hand to his forehead several times. 'You told my wife what happened? You stupid girl.'

'I'm leaving after payday. I can't work here anymore. The matron at my hostel knows about you. She suggested I report the incident to the police.'

Obviously, nothing like this had happened to my boss before.

The next day, being Friday, Ski gave me my pay packet without looking at me. With the money safely in my handbag, I stepped outside.

A police car rolled up and stopped at the door. *Had the matron of my hostel decided to take the matter into her own hands and inform the police of Podoski's sexual molestations?*

I rushed to the bus stop, hoping to avoid anyone who'd try to take advantage of me.

That was the last I saw of Ski.

***

I found myself jobless again. I couldn't write to Mum about it, as she'd worry. So I hid my disappointment and fears. *Should I have gone to England with my family?* A secure job was waiting for me there and I had my brothers to protect me.

A few days later, the Commonwealth Agency found me a position at the University of Western Australia as a dining-room maid at Currie Hall, with free board and lodging. My room was similar to the students' rooms, and since I intended to complete my studies, the situation proved ideal.

The staff was amongst the friendliest ever. Everyone was kind and helpful. At dinner time, the girl-in-charge would say, 'Hizel, lie the tible.'

By then, no longer confused by different accents, I understood what it meant.

Having arrived in Perth when the wild flowers were in bloom, I took the bus to King's Park on weekends and joined in the walks conducted by a park ranger. Enraptured at the sight of the carpets of flowers spread out in the distance, I enjoyed the visual feast and the sense of freedom that engulfed me.

Even as a dining-room maid, I earned more money than I had ever done in Burma. I bought a transistor with my first pay packet and listened to songs protesting about the war in Vietnam and others such as *Walk Like a Man, Eighteen Yellow Roses* and *Let's Twist Again*. Music filled my soul. Nothing tarnished my happiness—now complete and unalloyed. My cup of joy flowed over in waves. Joy had evaded me ever since the Japanese invasion of Burma had robbed me of the magic of childhood. I'd found inner peace with the nuns, but I'd never experienced the sheer happiness of being alive.

Not knowing the value of money, I dreaded the ordeal of shopping. In Burma, the shops had stood half empty and even a piece of material was rationed, and limited to only one member of the household; the others had to wait for their turn. Here in Perth, goods flowed out from the aisles to the pavements. The shop assistant at Ahearn's was most helpful, choosing the correct size bra and even fitting me, much to my embarrassment.

I received credit for four first year units and enrolled at the university as a second-year student to study English, History and Italian. Before 1967 came to a close, the nuns called me up for an interview at a Catholic

Girls' College at Victoria Square and I signed on for a teaching position in the following academic year. I wished for nothing better. My wave of joy swelled even higher. On weekends, I took half-day or full-day tours and visited well-known places in Perth and Fremantle. I loved life; loved everything and everyone in Perth.

As Christmas 1967 approached, my thoughts flashed back to my earliest memories of the day. I'd been put to bed earlier than usual because Santa was to visit us at mid-night. Next morning, my sister June woke me. A lovely rag doll looked down from a lucky stocking filled with balloons and parcels of various shapes and sizes. June received a beautiful shut-eye china doll with real shoes, as well as several packages. After opening our gifts, we raced downstairs to the lounge-room to show our presents to the rest of the family. Rupert was devouring a copy of *Boys' Own Annual*, and Bertie lay on the carpet with a meccano set. He had already built himself a bridge. Happy among mounds of coloured wrapping paper and cocoons of ribbon, June and I played with our new toys until breakfast. The table was laden with oranges, walnuts, and all kinds of sweets in their gay wrappings; and of course, a Christmas cake with the words, *Merry Xmas* in white icing.

At dinner, there was roast goose followed by plum pudding and mince pies. The day ended at the cinema with *The Christmas Carol*.

***

I particularly missed my family at Christmas-time. Because I knew no one else in Perth, at the time, the Samuels invited me over for Christmas dinner.

As the festive season in Perth faded away and the New Year grew older, I commenced teaching at Mercedes College, a Girls' College run by the Sisters of Mercy. It stood in the centre of Perth—across the road from St. Mary's Cathedral. The students were adorable, the salary better than I ever anticipated. My hostel was within five minutes walking distance from the college. I found friends there, and still keep in touch with some.

The move into town meant catching a bus for evening lectures at the university. This entailed bus trips along the shores of the Swan River—a relaxing break between teaching and study. I sat back in the seat, stretched out my legs and clasped my hands on my chest. The Swan Brewery illuminated like a ship, reminded me of a Tennyson poem. The words, '*the long light shakes across the lakes*', floated through my mind as I watched its reflection in the river. The bus terminus was at Irwin Street, only a short distance from my hostel. I was invariably the last passenger, and the friendly bus driver frequently struck up a conversation with me before I left.

'Where are you from?' he asked on my first trip back from the university.

'From Mandalay.'

He broke into a few strains of *The Road* to *Mandalay*...

How friendly the people of Perth were!

A Rip Van Winkle complex still persisted from years of incarceration as a teenager. It was as if I'd fallen asleep for a decade, only to awaken to another era. I went about noiselessly, walked demurely and remained in the background. I needed to learn to walk easily and freely, a difficult habit to break, since the Rule had held sway over all my thoughts and actions every minute of the day. Recalling that Rose had once criticised my walk, I paid for a course in deportment. Determined to cultivate those parts of my mind and body that remained undeveloped, I enrolled for lessons in swimming and Yoga, took up Jujitsu and learned the art of defending myself. My slender body began to take on curves with the good food and exercise. I looked directly into people's eyes without embarrassment and approached them with ease.

God blessed me with happiness. Submerged feelings, formerly mute, now erupted in a transport of rapture. Engrossed with studies, my head in the clouds with sheer happiness, I once again let world events pass by unnoticed—except when Neil Armstrong landed on the moon in July 1969. My thirst for knowledge remained insatiable. I intended to continue the search long after I sailed into port and found a pilot to man the helm. My soul sang with internal music.

Zane Grey's westerns made me dream of mounting a horse and riding off into the sunset. The only time I had ridden one was as a child in the foothills of the Himalayas, during a holiday in Darjeeling. Now, at weekends

I went horse-riding at John Forrest National Park with a friend from the hostel. The gentle rhythm of the horse's hooves and the rush of air on my cheeks filled me with inexpressible delight.

Days passed. I planned to travel overseas during the summer holidays when my studies were completed. Nothing would now stand in my way towards my goal of travel and adventure. I'd been parted from Mum for nearly a year now and dreamed of the time when I'd visit my family abroad.

But things were to turn out differently.

Chapter 24

The Family

I corresponded with my mother weekly, and opened a bank account in her name, depositing a fixed amount for her on pay days. Mum wrote saying she yearned for a warmer climate and would be happy to teach in Australia if her application for an entry permit was successful. As soon as I received her letter, I lost no time in finding her a position and sponsored her out to Australia.

After living in England for barely a year, Mum joined me in mid-January 1969. Her heart ached to leave her other three children back in England. She loved Bertie and had shed many bitter tears for him. As an infant, he'd been rejected by his father but Mum had found comfort in hearing him recite his favourite nursery rhymes. Later, as a young man, he saved us from our father's abuse by paying for our railway tickets and taking us to Mandalay.

Mum had a special bond with her youngest daughter—the first child she reared without the aid of a nanny. As a toddler of two, Rose nearly died from smallpox. Although half-starved during the war, like a mother pelican tearing at its own breast to feed its young with its life's blood, she had breastfed the sick infant. Her bonding with Rose had been forged through suffering, and her heart ached to leave her behind.

As for Winston, he was her pride and joy. Each time he'd been near death, a sword of sorrow pierced her. She loved him tenderly and been mother and father to him ever since she'd left her husband. Many times, my mother recalled the day he had a near-death experience. When out fishing with his mate, the boat capsized. As Winston sank to the bottom, he saw a ray of light above and heard the most beautiful celestial music. In a trance-like state, the music engulfed him. He felt himself being carried aloft on a bed of clouds, higher and higher until a strong illumination dazzled him.

Fortunately for my brother, his friend saved him. When consciousness returned, he blinked. His mate peered down at him. 'Thought we had lost you, mate.'

A few years later, Winston used up another of his nine lives, while working as a male nurse on an oil rig off the coast of Western Australia. His long hours prevented him from always being with his family, but he returned every ten days or so. The salary helped pay off the loan on his house. Pleased to accumulate a little nest egg, Winston worked hard, but unfortunately, the structure was damaged during a storm and the workers had to be hauled off by helicopters. Winston remained on board, his heart pounding against his ribs, until the last man had departed.

The oil rig sank minutes after the helicopter pulled him off to safety.

Winston wrote to me, describing these brushes with death. I thanked God for watching over my brother.

The harsh English winter had been too much for mum but Perth's warm weather revived her. She commenced work in the new academic year and loved her students. However, she tired easily and the job proved too demanding on her reserves of energy. She struggled on, not wishing to be a burden on us. I visited Mum every weekend, bringing her comfort and companionship, but she couldn't settle down and longed to be united with *all* her children.

Back in England, Rose and Winston made plans to follow Mum. They saw better prospects in Australia, so filled in the necessary papers, and I sponsored them out. A year later, my brother and sister boarded the *Oriana* for the trip 'Down Under' and arrived at Fremantle on Anzac Day.

Rose and Winston were drunk with happiness. Neither of them had been born when we went to Darjeeling in pre-war days. So this had been their first ocean voyage.

As soon as I met Rose at the Fremantle docks, she chattered on about the sea voyage. 'When our ship touched in at South Africa, we disembarked and went sight-seeing. I took a short train ride, and was amazed when a barrier went up in the train between whites and coloured.'

Winston nodded, then took up the conversation. 'When we docked at Aden, I bought what I thought was an excellent watch. After wandering around for a while, I checked the time. My watch wasn't working. Too late to return to the stall and confront the seller, I returned to the ship. Once on deck, I watched the shoreline receding, as the *Oriana* pulled away from Aden. The sweltering weather added to my irritation at being cheated. I flung the watch into the sea, and returned to my cabin, swearing I'd never allow myself to be conned again.' He cast me a mournful look.

He'd spent his hard-earned money and couldn't get over his loss. My mind returned to the time I'd escorted him to Rangoon before his departure for the United Kingdom. He'd grown now and was taller than me. His first employment was at the Swan Brewery. Later, he took up karate lessons, and earned a Black Belt in karate.

I was putting aside my savings for my long-cherished dream—a trip overseas. To build up my reserves, I worked as a waitress during the summer holidays. So I couldn't help either Winston or Rose financially. I found board and lodgings for my sister at the Girls' Friendly Society with me and took her to the swimming pool in our spare time. Very soon she obtained a teaching position, and left the hostel to prepare a home for Paddy and herself.

He arrived a few months later, and they married in October 1970. Rose looked beautiful in a white silk slack suit. It was a quiet wedding with only Mum, Winston and me in attendance. Bertie was still in England.

After the wedding Mum said, 'I'll die in peace if I could see all of you married, before I pass away.'

The Lord granted her prayers in a way no one could have dreamed of.

Chapter 25

Love

1968 ushered in a new way of life. The songs, *Dance to the Music* and *Honey*, reflected my mood. A page had turned, and the future rose before me like an immense panorama.

I continued my correspondence with Ralph. However, with the demands on my time the letters grew less frequent until they ceased altogether. I soon realised that my sentiments had been no more than a crush for an older man. A schoolgirl romance.

Within a year I was physically attracted to another man but it turned out to be simply a brief infatuation. My distrust of men made me shy away from the thought of marriage. I desired love, but the words I'd once read in a novel, *'a woman gives her heart and a man takes her body,'* kept cropping up.

'Believe me, I should know,' Mum said, when I spoke to her about it.

I buried the terrors of the past deep in the recesses of my mind and learned to sail my own ship, opting for adventure and travel rather than marriage. An upsurge of expeditionary fever possessed me. I hungered to explore this vast continent and savour the joys I'd missed during my teens. My older sister June had awakened the spirit of adventure within me long ago, and I could not wait to fly away on that magic carpet.

The end of the academic year loomed ahead. The long summer holiday stretched for six weeks, so I booked a coach trip to Adelaide, Melbourne and Sydney, planning to stop at the three capital cities.

As I crossed the Nullarbor, my soul vibrated with a hidden melody, keeping in tune with the wilderness of the desert. The spell was broken by the unwelcome advance of a passenger as he pressed his thigh against mine but I placed my handbag between us, crossed my arms over my chest and scowled. He laughed.

***

The world-famous rock musical, *Hair*, was showing in Sydney. Fortunately, while staying at the YWCA in central Sydney, I met Susan, who came from a small country town. She sat opposite me at breakfast. 'My name's Susan, Sue for short. Have you been to Sydney before?

'No. This is my first trip out of Perth.'

'I've been here a few times.' Sue looked at me over glasses that had slid down to the end of her slightly hooked nose. 'Have you seen *Hair* yet?'

'No. I'd love to but I'm scared to go on my own.'

Sue smiled. 'Me too. Let's go together. I'm dying to see it.'

Thrilled at the idea of being able to attend the smash hit with its shocking reputation, we set out to buy our tickets.

***

The following day, I visited the homes and gardens of pioneers like John Macarthur.

We left for Adelaide the next morning. From there, I took a coach tour to the Barossa Valley and given a window seat at the front, behind the driver. The seat next to me remained vacant. I can still visualise the events of that day as though it was only yesterday. My attention kept wandering to the footpath, but no one appeared to be getting on. Already the other seats were filling, and the one beside me continued to remain unoccupied.

At the last minute, a tall youth entered and sat next to me. The sun lit up his hair like spun gold. His forget-me-not-blue eyes shone as he smiled at me. Then he turned away and I caught a whiff of his aftershave. He wore a pair of faded blue jeans. His well-chiselled features reminded me of Roger Moore. Thrilled by his broad shoulders and tapering torso, my pulse raced. *Who is this good-looking young man? Possibly a university student on holiday.* My heart, an entrapped bird, flapped its wings. I tried to control my emotions. It proved an impossible task.

Before taking off, the coach captain checked our names against his passenger list. My companion's name was Colin.

I sat by the window watching the scenery, occasionally stealing a glance at my travelling companion. Once, I caught his eye. 'Isn't it a lovely day?'

He smiled and nodded. His reticence only served as a stimulus to me. Other men I had met on the trip had not hesitated to start chatting—sometimes being friendly, but more often trying to seduce me. Colin treated me with respect, and I sensed something different in him. He was shy and thoughtful.

We disembarked at the first Barossa Valley winery where the wine flowed freely. At the wine-tasting, I noticed with interest that Colin merely swirled it around in his mouth to sample its flavour. When the bus stopped again at the winery where we were to have our lunch, I found myself beside him as we entered the building.

His ears turned pink as he leant towards me. 'Would you like to join me for lunch?'

I beamed with delight and felt my own colour rising. 'I'd love that. Thank you.'

He drew up a chair for me at his table, his manner hovering between bashfulness and courtesy. He drank in moderation at the meal. Another plus in his favour, as my father had been a violent alcoholic.

We were drawn towards each other for the rest of the trip. After our last visit to the wineries, the coach captain, who had obviously noticed our growing friendship, asked, 'Are you two doing anything in particular this evening? You should see the sights of Adelaide at night. Go to Light's Vision.'

Colin studied his nails. 'I don't know where it is.'

Unable to still the furious beating of my heart, I gave him my copy of *This Week in Adelaide,* a booklet containing a map of Adelaide.

He looked at it. 'Have you been to the botanical gardens?' A rosy hue suffused his face.

'No, but I'd love to. Tomorrow's my last day in Adelaide.'

'It's my first day here. I drove from Canberra by car, and only took this tour because I didn't know the way to the Barossa Valley. May I pick you up at your hotel tomorrow morning? We'll go to the botanical gardens and then to Light's Vision.'

I felt my cheeks glow and my heart beat wildly. 'Yes, please.'

***

That night I lay awake for several hours, too excited to sleep. I thought of nothing else but the day's outing. Eventually I lapsed into a deep and refreshing slumber, only waking when the morning sun kissed the sleep from my eyes.

At the appointed time, Colin drove up in his blue Datsun and opened the door for me. Once again, the fragrance of his aftershave allured me. The interior of his car had the clean fresh smell of leather and the paintwork shone. Colin showed me the sights of Adelaide on our way to the botanical gardens. On our arrival, we wandered around in the park, lost in the beauties of nature. The breeze played hide-and-seek among the leaves while we immersed ourselves in our surroundings.

After our slow start the previous day, Colin now seemed at ease with subjects that interested him. He possessed a natural eloquence. Filled with a wild and joyous sweetness, I floated in the clouds with the handsome stranger, engrossed in his running commentary on the plants. Time galloped on and I lost hold of the reins.

The blue of a perfect summer day had not yet surrendered to dusk, and the sun filtered through the trees by the time we wandered back towards the car. When we arrived at the exit, the locked gates barred further progress. I was alone in the garden with a stranger! I glanced up at the tall and forbidding gate and shuddered. *What's going to happen now?*

My fears proved groundless. Seeing the distress on my face, Colin said, 'The walls are not very high. We can easily climb over.'

The surrounding stone walls upon which he leaped were about a metre in height. His outline, silhouetted against the backdrop of colours from the setting sun, revealed his lean, wiry body to advantage. His muscles rippled as he stretched his arms out and drew me up. Sweeping me off my feet, he set me down upon the wall. Then he alighted on the other side with the agility of a deer. Once more he stretched his arms out and lifted me down.

A wave of desire swept over me and my heart pounded furiously as he reached for my hand. His touch sent my pulse racing. A sense of intoxication mounted to my head and a never-to-be-forgotten bliss overwhelmed me. He held me captive. I trod on air as we walked hand-in-hand to the car, enveloped in the magic of that moment. Colin opened the door for me and drove in silence towards Light's Vision, a lookout on Montefiore Hill.

Still silent, we climbed to the top. A surge of pent-up feelings filled me with an inexpressible yearning as he held my hand within his. A stage with the life-size bronze statue of Colonel William Light as its centrepiece stood on the summit. The lights of Adelaide twinkled brightly, reflecting my joy as we surveyed the sweeping views of the city and its parklands. The evening gave birth to a latent sense of excitement. Colin stroked my hair and gazed at me. The soft sounds of the night were a wordless melody as he pressed his lips to mine. I returned his kiss and all the love bottled up within me broke their confines. Locked in his arms, I remained heedless of passers-by and soared far above Light's Vision. I could not live without him. He was the man of my dreams, my soul mate. A knight in shining armour, he would save me from the ivory tower in which I lived.

Our shyness fell away, loosening our tongues. We shared the little secrets of our childhood, the pleasures and pains. Colin was doing his final year in a Clerk of Works' Course. A member of the Canberra Rowing Club, he had won several prizes, racing on Lake Burley Griffin. We talked for hours and exchanged addresses and phone numbers, promising to write to each other. Then, hand-in-hand, we gazed silently upon the lights of Adelaide.

***

Barren and bare, the Nullarbor Plain stretched for two thousand kilometres. We shut all the windows to keep out the dust. Unfortunately, the shut windows also cut me off from the passing scenery. Knowing there was nothing but grey saltbush, I shut my eyes and thought of my wonderful time with Colin. *Will he really write to me or was it just a holiday romance?*

A blue envelope awaited me on my arrival home. In a transport of joy I pressed it to my lips, holding it to my cheek, living again the gentle caress of Colin's touch. I sat down, letting the contents of the letter sink in. Full of endearing words, it raised me to the pinnacle of ecstatic joy. We wrote every week, the letters nourishing our love until we could no longer cope with the distance separating us.

In late autumn, Colin invited me to meet his family during the school holidays. I loved him with all my heart but my constant worry was our age difference. *It does not matter so much now, but will he love me in ten, twenty or thirty years' time when I look old and ugly? Will he still care for me then?*

I took a bus to Mum's place and burst into her room. 'Colin has asked me over to meet his family. Should I go? He's much younger than me. What should I do?'

Mum was a woman of few words and liked to convey her messages by quoting the words from a book or singing a song. Whenever any of us quarrelled or sulked, she would sing:

> *Life's too short to quarrel.*
> *Hearts are too precious to break.*
> *Shake hands and let us be friends*
> *For old time's sake.*

When Bertie was leaving home, Mum sang:

> *You're going to leave the old home, Bert.*
> *Today you're going away.*
> *You're going amongst the city folks to dwell...*

Now, as I asked for her opinion, Mum smiled and replied in the great bard's words, 'It's better to have loved and lost, than never to have loved at all.'

Her advice removed the last vestiges of my doubt. I hugged her and immediately wrote to Colin telling him I would love to accept his offer. I scored each day off the calendar with trembling hands.

On the commencement of my vacation, the taxi could not drive fast enough to the airport and on my arrival, another long wait ensued before boarding the aircraft.

As the plane touched ground in Canberra, my pulse raced at the thought of seeing Colin again. I'm a Eurasian—a mixture of English, Portuguese, Persian, Indian and Burmese. Besides, I am a Catholic, and he, an Anglican. *Will his parents accept me? Will they be prejudiced against my colour, my race or my religion?*

Colin was at the airport. After driving to Lake Burley Griffin taking me for a walk to show me the carillon, he drove home and introduced me to his mum and dad.

His mother came forward to greet me. 'We're so glad our Colin has chosen well. His uncle is also a teacher.'

His father shook hands and his sister rushed out, holding a plate. A lump of ice glittered on it. It had snowed in Canberra a few days before, and she had saved a handful for me in the fridge, knowing I'd never seen snow!

An excellent guide, Colin showed me all the sights of Canberra. I listened to the musical chimes of the carillon and enjoyed the bright autumn colours of the trees. When weary, we sat beside the lake and I lay my head on his chest.

One idyllic evening towards the close of my holiday, while watching the sun set on Lake Burley Griffin he said, 'If I asked you to marry me, would you?'

My heart leapt. 'Of course, I would.'

Colin, with more confidence in his voice, whispered the age-old question, 'Will you marry me?'

Those four little words gave me the most joyous moment of my life. I threw both arms around him. 'Yes.'

The next day when I awoke, the grass sparkled with dew. After a hurried breakfast, we drove to the city centre and paused outside Proud's, admiring the beautiful diamond rings on white lace and black velvet. The shop was closed, so we peered into the window display, looking for a suitable ring as a pledge of our love for each other.

When the jeweller opened his doors, instead of going inside, Colin led me to the square and sat on a rustic seat beneath the plane trees. 'I need time to consider.'

Does he already have regrets? Is he thinking of backing out? I gazed at the trees in stunned silence, as if they would give me an answer. They had shed most of their leaves but richly coloured reds and golds still hung on. Time passed slowly. I counted each leaf as it fell. My heart throbbed as anxious thoughts raced through my brain. I sat beside him, longing to ask what he meant. I saw myself speaking and heard the words in my mind, but said nothing. I bit my lip, not knowing that Colin needed to ponder over things before making an important decision.

After a long silence, he rose. 'Let's go and select the ring.'

I followed him into the shop with a spring in my step. Then, without exchanging a word to each other, we pointed to the same ring—a diamond solitaire on a raised bed supported by two oval-shaped legs embedded with a tiny diamond in the centre.

Colin picked up the ring and watched it glint beneath the light. 'It suits your little hand.' He slipped it on my finger.

His mother lost no time in holding an engagement party for us. My first ever party! My heart sang. I still had another year to complete my degree, so we planned to marry after my graduation.

When the guests had departed, Colin said, 'This is the final year of my Clerk of Works Course. After I've completed my studies, I'll come to Perth to be near you.' He drew me to him and kissed me.

In the remaining few days, while the trees were still decked with their autumn foliage, Colin showed me Canberra at its best. Borne in the wings of romance, the soft breeze uplifted our hearts, melting us into tenderness. I sat on his lap while he rocked me in his arms and stroked my hair.

The days passed all too quickly and when the hour arrived for my flight back to Perth, I could scarcely tear myself away from him. I cried the whole way back. *Who said that parting is such sweet sorrow? It is heart-wrenching*!

The love letters in their blue envelopes now came in daily. I couldn't wait for the summer holidays when Colin would come to Perth. Consumed with longing for each other, we watched the same moon at nights. Simon and Garfunkel's *Bridge over Troubled Waters* and Gilbert O'Sullivan's *Alone Again* were popular at the time. We listened to the same songs on the radio, meditating over the same words.

When the academic year came to a close and Colin had completed his studies at college, he packed all his belongings in his Datsun Bluebird, and drove across the dusty Nullarbor.

***

Perth was in a slump at that time. Colin trudged from place to place to seek employment, but work was unavailable.

A representative of the Builders' Union shook his head. 'Go back to Canberra where you have job security.'

Colin returned from the interview looking despondent. 'A Union rep has advised me to return to Canberra where I have a good position as a foreman. If I remain here, I'll be dependent on you. Will you come with me to Canberra? We'll marry as soon as the banns are ready and you could study as an external student.' It was obvious he'd thought it all out carefully.

Neither of us could bear to be separated from each other again, so the only alternative was for me to join him in Canberra. Although sorely disappointed I'd be leaving her, Mum was overjoyed at the prospect of a happy marriage for me. Colin invited my family to a farewell dinner at King's Park, knowing they would be unable to attend my wedding.

The next morning, we left Perth, returning to Canberra via Albany and Esperance. The Pink Lakes were as rosy as the first blush of dawn.

Delighted at his return, Colin's parents made preparations for our wedding. We approached the parish priest, Father O'Shea, who instructed us in the duties of a married couple.

To my great joy, Colin said, 'I know your beliefs mean a lot to you, and I'm certain we'll get more from our lives if we are of the same faith.' He made all the necessary arrangements and was baptised in the Catholic faith before we pledged our vows.

We married on 12 February 1971, in St Xavier's Church. In spite of the short notice, thirty-two guests were present. Bertie was still in England at the time and wasn't able to come over for my wedding.

Colin's sister, Sally, was bridesmaid, and his close friend, Jim O'Brien, was best man. I would have loved one of my brothers to give me away, but having already spent most of their savings when moving from England to Perth, Winston, like the rest of my family, wasn't able to attend the wedding.

A Dutch gentleman, an old friend of Colin's dad, gave me away. I was dressed in white, and Colin looked so handsome in a dark suit as we pronounced our vows. I had never dreamed of such joy. Colin had led me from dreams to reality, from sipping the nectar of life to drinking a full draught of delight. We loved each other with a strong and passionate, yet tender love and looked forward to a long and happy life with each other and our children.

Chapter 26

Canberra, 1971

We spent our honeymoon at Wombean Caves and slept under a canopy of stars surrounded by majestic rocky hills. It excelled any wedding suite at the grandest hotel. Those precious days remain like a mosaic in my memory.

After the honeymoon, we moved into a small but comfortable unit in Queanbeyan. Unlike so many young couples, we refrained from buying a television at the outset of our marriage; happy in our embraces, often in silence; at other times sharing our dreams. Love and romance filled our days. We wrote little notes to each other, leaving them in conspicuous places. Our love grew stronger as the days went by. We had the same dream, the same spirit of adventure.

Colin did not let our hearts rule our minds and frequently said, 'First things, first. We must build a house.'

We purchased a block of land in one of the newer suburbs of Canberra, and Colin drew up a plan for our home. In the evenings and on weekends he dug the foundations, labouring on our block every evening and on weekends. I did my bit, mixing the mortar and wheeling the barrow to him. On one occasion when he was felling a tree in the garden with an axe, it began to lean towards him, and, fearing he'd be crushed, I jumped onto its path to take the brunt of its fall. He flung away his axe, grabbed me and sprang out of the way. Fortunately, his quick action saved us both from serious injury. We laughed about it afterwards.

Not long after, I found employment as a kitchen maid and spent the whole day scrubbing pots and pans and cleaning the oven at a hotel. By the end of the year, I was admitted into the Public Service and, upon my graduation, I was promoted to Graduate Clerk. My salary increased and I received a refund of my university fees.

The cheque arrived in time for Colin to pitch the roof over the house and bring our home to lock-up stage. It entitled us to receive the first instalment of the government loan.

Things moved swiftly after that. The money paid for an electrician, plumber and plasterer, and brought our home to near completion.

***

Rose and Pat drove over from Perth in their van and visited us at our flat on their way for a holiday in New Zealand. I secretly wished they'd come after we'd moved into our new home, so they could stay with us. But they had now saved sufficient funds and probably wanted a break before they started their own family.

Unfortunately, we were unable to offer them accommodation in our little bedsitter, so they parked in our garage and had breakfast with us. Later, we took them to our block where we had a picnic lunch. After our meal, Colin wandered off with Pat to show him how far he'd progressed with the building.

While we were alone, Rose said, 'Dad was admitted in an insane asylum for treatment. I've brought you a copy of his last letter to me.' Then she handed it to me.

207/12
Yankinmyo
December 18

Dear Rose,

I'm not sure that I can still write English, but if you find mistakes please don't put it down to insanity. I don't think I have to fear a repetition. God is Great. The fact is, I now have very little chance of using both written and spoken English. All that I now have to read at home is Law Yone's Burmese!

It is no use my telling you that though I have not written to any of you for a very long time. Mum and my children come to my thoughts every day of my life. I now have a little baby with features almost exactly like Trevor's and even the way the right foot stamps on the ground in temper is identical. The big eyes are Mum's or Winston's and the little mouth is yours – don't be angry with me, but what I have said is the truth.

Well, Rose I wish all of you a very, very happy X'mas and equally happy New Year, and may God continue to bless all.

Closed with all my love,
Dad

My father had been brilliant in English and loved reading. What a terrible thing it must have been to have been deprived of books. *Why had neither Mum, Bertie or Rose told me about his time in a mental institution? Perhaps it was because of the stigma attached to mental illness in those days.*

Thanks to my sister showing me the letter, I found it easier to shed the burden of hatred I had carried from my teenage years and through my convent days.

God's healing grace finally penetrated my soul and enabled me to forgive my father's past misdeeds.

***

On the drive back to the flat, I pointed out the Canberra hospital to Rose, and said, 'That is where our baby will be born.'

Those prophetic words were to come true sooner than we expected. Before the year had passed, I sent away for a 'Baby Bundle' and knitted a little blue outfit for our baby, who was due in September.

One night as we lay in bed, aware of a faint movement within me, taking Colin's hand in a rush of emotion, I placed it on the spot. 'I want a boy—a boy who looks like you.'

We were thrilled to feel the baby's movement. *In a few months' time, we'll have the little one in our arms!*

We lay awake, glowing with anticipation of a bright and happy future. A rosy road stretched out before us. Immersed in a sea of love, my past sufferings and unhappiness were sluiced away. I lay in exquisite bliss within the circle of Colin's arm and thought of my traumatic childhood. Those unhappy days had led me to Australia and brought me to him. The Prince Charming of my dreams had rescued me, and all my youthful visions had now been realised. I had longed for the wonderful and received the sublime.

I thought of what the priest had said to me, years back about marrying a good man. In retrospect, they were prophetic words: *You have given several years of your life to God, and He will reward you with a good husband.*

How true it is that God rewards one a hundredfold!

Epilogue

My love for Colin grew with each succeeding year. We flew over to Perth several times, and travelled to Europe and the UK to meet his relatives, thus fulfilling my dreams of travel.

My brother Bertie came to live in Perth to be near Mum. After settling down, he drove over to see us in our new home. Little Winston also visited us in Canberra. We all now lived in our adopted country, although in opposite sides of the continent.

Colin and I paid for my mother's flights to Canberra, and I was united with Mum on two separate occasions before she passed away.

By God's grace, even my childhood dream came to pass when Part One of my Memoir, *Heaven Tempers the Wind. Story of a War Child* was published by Armour Books in 2016. Within a month, *Chocolate Soldier— The Story of a Conchie* was released by Rhiza Press.

Part Two of my memoir, *The Sides of Heaven*, is in your hands and Part Three, written from Colin's perspective, will hopefully be out very shortly.

www.ingramcontent.com/pod-product-compliance
Lightning Source LLC
Chambersburg PA
CBHW021104080526
44587CB00010B/369